Teach
Yourself

Get that Job with
the Right CV

Julie Gray

For UK order enquiries: please contact Bookpoint Ltd,
130 Milton Park, Abingdon, Oxon OX14 4SB.
Telephone: +44 (0) 1235 827720. Fax: +44 (0) 1235 400454.
Lines are open 09.00–17.00, Monday to Saturday, with a 24-hour
message answering service. Details about our titles and how to
order are available at www.teachyourself.co.uk

Long renowned as the authoritative source for self-guided learning –
with more than 50 million copies sold worldwide – the **Teach Yourself**
series includes over 500 titles in the fields of languages, crafts, hobbies,
business, computing and education.

British Library Cataloguing in Publication Data: a catalogue record
for this title is available from the British Library.

First published in UK 2010 by Hodder Education, part of Hachette
UK, 338 Euston Road, London NW1 3BH.

The **Teach Yourself** name is a registered trade mark of
Hodder Headline.

Typeset by MPS Limited, A Macmillan Company.

Printed in Great Britain for Hodder Education, an Hachette
UK company, 338 Euston Road, London NW1 3BH,
by CPI Cox & Wyman, Reading, Berkshire RG1 8EX.

The publisher has used its best endeavours to ensure that the URLs
for external websites referred to in this book are correct and active
at the time of going to press. However, the publisher and the author
have no responsibility for the websites and can make no guarantee
that a site will remain live or that the content will remain relevant,
decent or appropriate.

Hachette UK's policy is to use papers that are natural, renewable
and recyclable products and made from wood grown in sustainable
forests. The logging and manufacturing processes are expected to
conform to the environmental regulations of the country of origin.

Impression number   10 9 8 7 6 5 4 3 2 1

Year   2014 2013 2012 2011 2010

Front cover: © Steve Cole/Photodisc/Getty Images

Back cover: © Jakub Semeniuk/iStockphoto.com, © Royalty-Free/Corbis,
© agencyby/iStockphoto.com, © Andy Cook/iStockphoto.com,
© Christopher Ewing/iStockphoto.com, © zebicho – Fotolia.com,
© Geoffrey Holman/iStockphoto.com, © Photodisc/Getty Images,
© James C. Pruitt/iStockphoto.com, © Mohamed Saber – Fotolia.com

Photo credits: p. 16: © PhotoAlto; p. 44: © Ingram Publishing Limited;
p. 98: © Ingram Publishing Limited; p. 158: © Stockbyte/Photolibrary
Group Ltd; p. 202: © PhotoAlto; p. 234: ©Photodisc/Getty Images;
p. 268: © Stockbyte/Photolibrary Group Ltd

Contents

Meet the author   **ix**
Foreword   **xi**
Only got a minute?   **xii**
Only got five minutes?   **xvi**
Only got ten minutes?   **xxiv**
1 How this book can help you   **1**
   Competition for jobs   1
   What is a CV?   2
   How can *I* write a CV?   3
   The benefits of writing your own CV   3
   Hard evidence   4
   CVs as personal trainers   5
   A personal CV   5
   Cost-cutting CVs   6
   Realistic CV   7
   Getting the most out of this book   8
   Where to start   9
   What about using a professional CV writer?   11
   Take your time   11
   When should I start my CV?   12
   Ten things to remember   14

Part one: Preparing the details   **17**
2 Getting the basic details together   **19**
   Personal details   19
   Personal information   23
   Education   26
   Career, employment or work history   28
   Your first job   30
   Voluntary work   30
   Write what you did   31
   Professional qualifications and memberships   36

Further skills and training   36
Interests   38
References   39
Beware!   42
Ten things to remember   43

Part two: Writing the basics   **45**
3   What skills do you have?   **47**
What makes you attractive?   47
Make it personal   47
Prove yourself   48
Building your Employment section   48
What everyone wants   52
Top ten generic skills   52
Convince an employer of your skills   63
Actions speak louder than words   64
Specialist skills   66
Ten things to remember   68
4   How to SHORTlist your best points   **69**
What makes a good example?   69
How do I SHORTlist my examples?   70
Specific   70
Honest   71
Outcome   72
Realistic   74
Transferable   76
Starting with your own examples   77
Ten things to remember   80
5   Prioritizing the essentials   **81**
Time constraints   81
Knowledge constraints   83
Start as you mean to go on   83
Converting SHORTlisted examples into a summary   84
Bulleted summary   87
Prose summary   88
'I' or 'he/she'?   89
Be consistent   92
Ten things to remember   94

Part three: Refining your language   **97**
6   Effective language to make you stand out   **99**
The basic rules of CV writing   100
Why action words matter   100
Refining your action words   102
Power action words   102
Present vs. past tense   107
Refining your adjectives   108
Use your power carefully   110
Use power where it counts   110
Avoid repetition   111
Reducing word count, not power   112
Refining/adding power   115
Ten things to remember   117
7   True lies: when marketing becomes deceit   **118**
Education lies   118
Employment lies   119
Other lies   119
What's the worst that can happen?   120
When does a stretch become a lie?   121
What if I'm just not good enough?   121
Do I have to be honest about everything?   122
If I can't lie, what can I do?   123
Ten things to remember   124
8   Honest spin: handling problem areas   **125**
Gaps in employment   126
Mind the gap   126
Temporary employment   129
Brief employment   131
How to use honest SPIN   132
Work on your 'story'   133
Work on your positive story   136
Reason for leaving   139
Employer criticism   139
Employment tribunals   140
Rehabilitation of offenders   140
Concealing a spent conviction   141
Convictions that are not spent   142

Illness 143
Proof 145
Disability 145
General rules for explaining gaps 146
Mind your language 146
Looking beyond your CV 147
Ten things to remember 148
9 Jargon: when to include, explain or avoid 149
What is jargon? 149
Rules for jargon 151
Job titles 155
Ten things to remember 156

Part four: Targeting it carefully 159
Professionally written CVs 160
Target your CV every time 161
10 Being specific (1) – targeting an industry 163
Understand what the sector expects 163
Be genuinely enthusiastic about the field you are
    trying to get into 164
Follow industry expectations 165
Lengths of specialist CVs 171
Which type of CV to use 174
Converting chronological CVs into other formats 176
Employment gaps 182
A final word on format 182
Ten things to remember 184
11 Being specific (2) – targeting a job and employer 185
The role 185
Skills and competencies 185
Automated scanning software 188
Reverse chronological CVs 191
Functional CVs 193
All CVs 193
The employer 194
Your reason for applying 197
Protect yourself 199
All research is useful 199
Ten things to remember 200

Part five: Presenting it perfectly   **203**
12 Layout – how should a finished CV look?   **207**
     Making your CV legible   207
     Text alignment   211
     The reasoning behind the rules   212
     Making your CV scannable (not the same as
     automated scanning!)   213
     Readability   216
     Quality control   220
     Ten things to remember   223
13 Format – factors to consider   **224**
     Why paper?   224
     Digital CVs   226
     Non-standard CV formats   227
     CVs for overseas applications   229
     The Europass CV format   230
     Ten things to remember   232

Part six: Using it properly   **235**
14 Complementing your CV: covering letters and
application forms   **237**
     Covering letters   237
     What type of covering letter should you use?   238
     What to include in a covering letter   238
     Don't just repeat, enhance   242
     Covering emails   245
     Speculative cover letters/emails   246
     Targeting your covering letter   246
     Application forms   250
     Personal statements or competency statements   252
     Ten things to remember   254
15 Living up to your great CV at interview   **255**
     You wrote it yourself   255
     You have pulled together proof of everything you claim   256
     You have worked on your positive spin to cover
     problem areas   257
     You've been honest   258
     One thing to remember   259

16 CV maintenance **260**
    Your CV is alive 260
    Regular CV checkups 261
    CV update checklist 262
    Incorporate feedback 264
    Be prepared 266
    Ten things to remember 267

Part seven: Further help **269**
17 Enhancing your employability – when nothing
   else works **271**
    Room for improvement 271
    Getting in early 272
    Time management 274
    One thing to remember 276
18 Further resources **277**
    Teach yourself CV writing online 277
    The CV Centre – online 278
    Teach Yourself books 278
    Index **279**

Meet the author

Any CV can be made to sparkle if you get two things right: language and layout. Sounds too simple? Well, it's exactly what professional CV writers do for their clients every day – and with amazing results. Good writing can transform an entire CV, making it sound more purposeful and positive, while great presentation hauls your best points into the spotlight.

My own experience comes from both sides of the fence. I wrote my first CV relatively late, already 19, for a dream sales job with a company car. Three years later I waved goodbye to the Vauxhall Cavalier after landing a job in a recruitment agency, where I developed my appreciation for well-crafted CVs. I sourced and interviewed candidates, tailoring their CVs to suit specific opportunities. Working with the same clients again and again was a great incentive to write glowing yet realistic CVs which sold candidates strongly, but which they could live up to. By applying the same skills I was able to move into trade marketing myself before I finally quit corporate life to become a freelance, specializing in something I felt I'd become pretty good at: CV writing. Since then I've helped more than 400 people, from school leavers to managers, to improve their image on paper and win over potential employers.

It's my belief that anyone can learn how to do what a good CV writer does. To have a powerful CV you don't need to be an experienced business executive, nor do you have to pay someone else a fortune to write it. All you need is some simple techniques, the time to ask yourself the right questions and the patience to refine your answers until they shine.

It's a widely known fact that how you talk about yourself often carries more weight than your actual ability. No, that doesn't mean you should fiddle your exam grades or invent qualifications, jobs and promotions to order. Untruths and exaggerations might make you feel more confident but they don't add real power to a CV – plenty of intelligent, skilled executives have appalling CVs – and lying only works against you in the long run. This book focuses instead on helping you change how you think, write and talk about yourself. It is possible to convince recruiters you are worth employing and still keep a clear conscience.

I realized many years ago that people whose CVs get them invited to job interviews are rarely 'naturally gifted' writers. They're often not the most skilled or experienced applicants either. The CVs that generate interviews are sent in by people who appreciate the simple fact that words, and how you use them, really do matter.

Julie Gray

Foreword

Dear Reader,

I have known Julie Gray for quite some time. I founded The CV Centre in 1998 and made the wise decision to hire Julie very early on. We have worked together ever since; she is now one of my Senior Consultants and The CV Centre is now the UK's leading CV consultancy.

As a professional CV writer, Julie sees every single day which CVs really achieve results. This puts her in an excellent position to help you to create a truly exceptional CV of your own. She tells you exactly what to put in, exactly what to leave out, and what kind of a 'spin' to put on your CV, to ensure that it will stand right out from the competition.

Never forget that getting it right is the difference between getting your foot in the door for an interview, or ending up in the 'no thank you' pile – also known as the bin! Getting it right is absolutely essential if you are to achieve your full career potential.

No matter what your age, background, job and level of experience, Julie can help you to create a CV that really works for you.

This book condenses the same proven methodology we use every day with our clients and contains all the tips and – dare I say it – tricks, that you need. Julie cuts through all the debate and opinion about CVs and shows you what really works from the recruiter's point of view – what we have *proved* to work.

I wish you the very best of luck in your future career. Reading this book will undoubtedly help to maximize your chances of success.

Kind regards,

James Innes

James Innes
Managing Director, The CV Centre
Author: *The CV Book; The Interview Book; Brilliant Cover Letters*

Only got a minute?

If you've got one minute to read this, you're spending longer than many recruiters will spend reading your CV. That doesn't mean it's not worth learning to write one – in fact the opposite is true. Teaching yourself to write an effective CV, instead of sending a poor quality one or paying someone else to write it, has enormous benefits beyond increasing your chances of getting an interview. The writing process itself can help to improve your understanding of employers' needs, awareness of your own skills, communication style, presentation and confidence.

Words matter

The words you use say a lot about you: they can give insight into your attitudes, beliefs and strengths, hopes, fears and weaknesses. They can also cause misunderstandings. A CV must be clear: convincing yet impressive, concise yet alluring, and true to who you are. The key is to be positive, while always thinking about things from a recruiter's perspective.

Build a factsheet

Your starting point is building your factsheet. This contains all the information you might need including personal details, qualifications and employment dates. Understanding what employers need and want to know is essential, as well as knowing which things you can (or indeed should) leave out.

Look at your skills

Spend time analysing your own skills. Identify which skills you have and think up concrete examples of when you've put these skills to good use and what the result was. Examples can come from paid or unpaid work, interests or personal life. Useful techniques like SHORTlisting (see Chapter 4) can help you to distil these into short, punchy bullet points.

Create a generic CV

Set the tone for your CV with a brief summary or profile, based on the skills you've identified. Add your objectives and that's your draft 'generic' CV – the foundation for all that follows. Your time and effort is then best spent honing your language and adding power.

Refine, refine, refine

- ▶ Your words ... to suggest a person of action, with purpose, who delivers benefits.
- ▶ Your sentences ... to keep them short, meaningful and relevant.
- ▶ Your section order ... to keep 'what you offer an employer' firmly in the spotlight.

Always remind the reader why they should be interviewing *you*.

Target

The final edit is your most important: targeting or tailoring your CV. Showing an employer you don't want just any job, but this one in particular, working for them. Do your research, and explain clearly why the fit between you, this role and this employer is so perfect. Target covering letters and application forms the same way.

Layout and presentation

Once the writing is finished, this takes over; it must be as strong as your CV content. Select the layout and format that feels right. Always do a quality check before sending. Keep your CV up to date and consider other (practical) ways to improve its basic content.

That's it. Time to get started. Teach yourself a valuable new skill: how to write a great CV.

5 Only got five minutes?

If you've got five minutes to read this, you're taking about five times as long as a typical recruiter will to read your CV. That doesn't mean you should invest an equal amount of effort in writing it, although many CVs look as though that's what happened.

A poor CV doesn't mean you are a poor employee. Brilliant senior managers and experienced leaders frequently turn out disappointing CVs while school leavers and graduates may excel. Weak CVs tend to result from a lack of knowledge, skill or effort.

If you truly lacked effort it's unlikely you'd be reading this, so it's probably safe to say this book is targeted at anyone who feels they lack sufficient knowledge or skill to write themselves a powerful CV. Fortunately, you can teach yourself both.

You will be guided through a writing process: a way of picking out the most relevant information from your mind and then refining it, again and again, until it makes the impact you deserve. Aimed at all levels of CV writer, the focus is on getting your language right before moving on to layout and overall presentation.

Hard copy

There's no doubt about it, writing is the hardest way you can communicate. No tone of voice, gesture or facial expression can help you to clarify your meaning and make sure someone understands you properly. Words, just words, on paper or screen. Words that a reader can interpret any way they choose.

Have you ever taken offence at an email, only to find the sender didn't mean it the way you thought? Or got a text reply you weren't expecting because the recipient misunderstood your text? When something like this happens, you normally have an opportunity to resolve the situation but when a potential employer misses the point or misunderstands you, it's too late. Your CV is in the bin and there is no second chance.

Write right

Your writing needs to be spot on right from the very start of your CV. It should attract and then hold the reader's attention until they have read and understood enough about you to put you on their interview shortlist. Powerful CVs need to be impressive yet thoroughly convincing, concise yet still inviting – and, above all, a true reflection of your best points.

With time and some guidance, you can learn to write a powerful CV. The key is to think positively and to evaluate everything from a recruiter's perspective instead of your own.

In their shoes

A common complaint from recruiters is that, when writing their CV, the applicant didn't take into account what the employer wanted. Yet, strangely enough, that's the whole point of your CV: to show an employer that you understand what's required and that you meet those requirements.

Employers need you to prove how you can be of benefit to their business: can you save them time, work hard, increase sales, be accurate, manage risk, develop staff, save money, motivate colleagues, meet targets or make a profit?

The most important word in the sentence above is 'prove': employers need reassurance that you are not making empty claims. Keep that in mind while writing, and you'll be well on your way to creating an employer's dream CV.

Preparation

A little preparation always helps writing flow more easily. There are certain basic facts, figures and dates you will always need on a CV: dates worked, certificates for qualifications, letters of commendation or promotion, etc. Find these first, keep them safe, and use them to create a basic, accurate factsheet to refer to – not just during your CV writing but throughout your job hunt.

Generic and specialist skills

If you're not sure what you're good at, let alone how to prove it to someone, focus on the types of skills that every employer will value. These ten generic skills are explained in detail along with examples and will help you kick start the process of assessing your own skills.

Once you find a skill on the list that you're good at, your next challenge is to think of concrete examples of how and when you've shown that skill, and the benefit it had. Examples can come from your work or (if you have little recent work experience) your personal life. Useful exercises like SHORTlisting (see Chapter 4) will help you distil these examples into brief, punchy bullet points: solid proof that you can place throughout your CV.

Once you've finished the generic skills list, you can move on to more specialist skills – and by now you'll have got the hang of it. Every example you can think of is potential proof to an employer that the claims in your CV are genuine.

Claiming three skills you can demonstrate is more powerful than claiming ten skills that you can't.

Start as you mean to go on

All the proof of skills you're putting into your Employment History is great stuff, but however concise you are this can easily get lost among the other words. A useful way around this is to draft a summary Profile and Objective at the start of your CV, which highlights your best points.

Working backwards from your skill examples, you'll find you can create a Profile and Objective quickly and easily. Find a style you're comfortable with, and by now you've effectively written your draft 'generic' CV. A generic CV should never, ever end up on a recruiter's desk – but it is the basis of everything else you will write.

The remainder of the book – and the majority of your time spent CV writing – is about honing content, language and style until this generic CV is as sharp as it can be. Incredibly, most people don't bother doing this part but it's what gives a CV real competitive edge. You will need that edge if you are to get interviews.

Be your own employer

Refining the language in your CV takes place in several stages, and each stage creates another layer of appeal. When you do this effectively, your CV sends the right messages.

The right words can suggest a person who takes action. One who is purposeful, intentional, knowingly takes control and delivers results.

The right phrasing reflects not just your skills but your personality, attracting employers in a way that's unique to you.

The right sentences are short but clear, making your CV totally readable, quick to understand and instantly memorable.

The right structure keeps the spotlight on what you have to offer an employer, and makes it easy for them to find what they are looking for. All the way through it reminds them why they should interview you, and not someone else who has similar experience.

You may think it strange to spend so long refining the language in your generic CV, but this is what will really lift it up above every other. Language holds enormous power.

Be unique

A refined generic CV is rather like a finely polished piece of wood: it has natural beauty, but no one is going to spend very long looking at it and it isn't memorable. Once you take this piece of wood and carve a unique sculpture from it, people start to pay attention.

Not only should your CV be unique compared to other people's CVs, but every one you send should be different. Yes, every one. Just like handmade sculptures, no two applications you send should ever be identical – each CV should be carved from your generic CV according to the job or employer in question.

Flattery gets you everywhere

This final edit is the most important one: targeting (or tailoring) your CV. Many people talk about doing this, but very few ever actually do it properly.

Targeting is not just about mentioning an employer's name somewhere in your CV and shuffling your sales and marketing experience nearer to the top of your Skills list.

Targeting is the art of showing an employer that you don't just want any job, you want this one, working for them: explaining why there is such a great fit between you and them.

To target your CV effectively, you do need a certain amount of knowledge about the marketplace, the company and the role you are applying for. If you don't have this knowledge, then take the time to do some research.

To convince an employer that you're the one for them, you need to think just as seriously about how best to convince an employer that they're the one for you. Who wouldn't welcome an employee who longs to work for them? Weave these arguments into every section of your targeted CV.

Finishing touches

Only when the writing is done should layout or presentation take over. These aspects might come last for practical reasons, but it doesn't diminish their importance in any way.

Layout and presentation must be as strong as your CV content. For some areas there are guidelines you should follow whereas for others you can express your preferences; it's up to you to create a professional-looking layout and format that you feel comfortable with, while avoiding common mistakes.

Your finished CV must be legible, quick to read and with key details easy to pick out. It should also be perfect in that there are no mistakes: you may need to enlist some help.

A skill for life

The book doesn't end with your completed CV. It will need to be
sent out with a covering letter and perhaps an application form,
maybe even a personal statement, and all these items need careful
targeting too.

Fortunately the information from your generic CV will also form
the basis of anything that accompanies your targeted CV, and the
writing techniques are all the same.

Once your application is checked and posted, the interview is over
and the job has been offered and accepted, that's still not the end
of it. Whatever may once have been the case, jobs are not lifelong
companions: your generic CV needs to be kept up to date.

Regular checks and revisions are an essential part of good CV
writing, just as assessing and developing your skills is a sensible
way to manage your career.

Start now

You can never start too early or be too prepared for writing your
own CV. The sooner you start, the greater your advantage over
people who aren't thinking about theirs yet.

Looking for a job is not a lottery. It's not about playing a numbers
game and hoping luck is on your side. Job hunting is a competition
and, like any competition, you will gain the upper hand by
studying, training, practising and ensuring you stay in good shape.

If you're worried about the future, why not teach yourself CV
writing today?

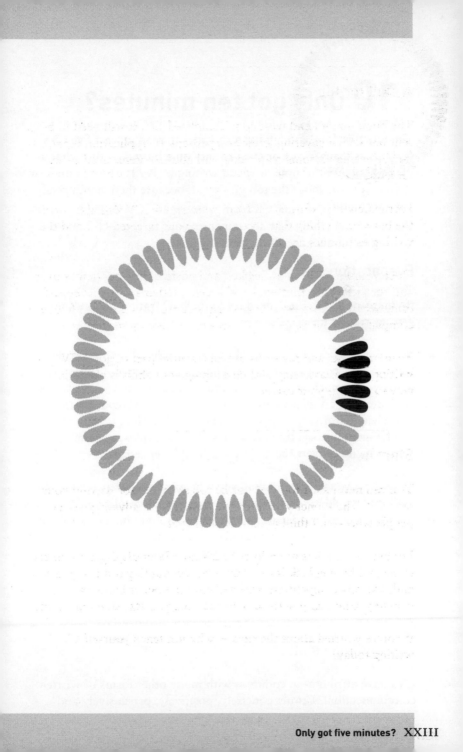

10 Only got ten minutes?

Ten minutes: long enough for a recruiter to read at least five CVs, perhaps as many as ten or even twenty on a busy day. But what's the right amount of time to spend writing a CV? It depends on how serious you are about the job you want, because there aren't really any shortcuts.

Preparation

If you want a CV, you'll need to do the preparation – there's no getting around it.

If you're short of time you might have considered simply asking someone else to write it for you. How much time would that save you? Not as much as you might think, when you consider a writer can't create a CV in a vacuum. You still need to provide all the underlying information: personal details, education, qualifications, employment history, track record, skills and evidence of them, achievements, advert for desired job, employer research, etc.

By the time you've done all that, you'd be most of the way through this book and would have a skeleton CV prepared. Hopefully you'd have already skimmed out details that weren't relevant or didn't add to your case. The only missing parts would be to do with refining the language you use and getting the layout right, the two aspects a CV writer could possibly help you with. Then again, you could learn to handle these elements yourself and thereby add a useful skill to your other talents.

Developing a skill

CVs have attributes in common with many other forms of written communication. Writing concisely, positively, persuasively and with relevance is a generally desirable trait: learning to do this for your CV could also benefit you in many other areas of your work.

Sending a good CV to an employer is also all the proof they need that your written communication skills are as excellent as you claim: they hold the evidence in their hands.

Thinking differently

Core to teaching yourself how to write a good CV is changing the way you think, write and talk about your capabilities.

Thinking differently doesn't mean adopting a feel-good, tell-yourself-you-are-wonderful-in-the-mirror-every-morning kind of way. It means using a logical framework to understand what skills are important to employers, which of them you're good at and, most importantly, how best to prove it on your CV.

As a side-effect, your self-belief will probably increase naturally as you go through this process. It can be quite hard to write about yourself confidently if, deep down, you don't think you are anything particularly special. You may feel this way because you don't really know what's expected of you, or you've had repeated rejections using your current CV.

This book can help you see that the things which come most easily to you – and which you therefore tend not to place so much value on – are often important skills that other people envy and an employer would appreciate. Your talent for keeping people calm perhaps, or your ability to work out solutions that suit everyone. So don't skip this step: take the time to consider all your possible strengths and how you demonstrate them. You may have more than you thought.

Once you're in this frame of mind, and are focused on proving all your skills, the way you write about yourself will improve automatically.

Writing differently

Good writing is very rarely perfect first time. Even the most experienced novelist will write a first draft, then a second, followed by much editing. They'll go through this process more than once. They'll likely rewrite several chapters, maybe even delete some completely, and then edit everything again. Finally, they are done. Their manuscript is sent to their editor, whose feedback may be incorporated into it as well.

Very few people go to this kind of trouble with their CV. Yet why wouldn't they? World fame and six-figure contracts don't come to most novelists. It's fair to say that a two-page CV could, by helping you land the job you want or need, generate far more income for you in just one year than a whole book can for an author. A book costs the reader less than a tenner, while employers are prepared to stake thousands of pounds on what they read in your CV. So why on earth do so many people expect their CV to be perfect first time?

If you haven't rewritten and revised your CV at least four or five times, then you probably haven't given it as much attention as you should. Rewriting doesn't mean you're a bad writer; it makes you a better one. Some people don't bother rewriting or editing their CV because they feel they don't have time. That's down to motivation.

For others, it's because they don't really know what to change to make it any better. That's something you can teach yourself how to do.

The main focus of this book is on writing, refining and targeting (another kind of rewriting) because these processes are so very fundamental to the success of your CV. Again, there is a logical framework to follow.

Writing CVs

At the initial writing stage, the emphasis is on putting in what every employer wants to see – proof.

Proof of your generic skills comes from your past actions. Examples of things you've done and the positive results you achieved. It's usually best to do nothing but write at this stage; don't try to evaluate the quality of the examples you are writing, just capture all your ideas on paper or on screen.

Your first set of revisions will be completed with the aid of a useful technique called SHORTlisting (see Chapter 4). Each example of your generic skills needs to meet several criteria, which you can check off as you build them in:

- ▶ Short (as it says on the tin)
- ▶ Honest (you be the judge)
- ▶ Outcome (the benefit of your actions)
- ▶ Realistic (i.e. believable)
- ▶ Transferable (useful to any role/employer).

SHORTlisted examples make for convincing proof.

You'll then do the same for the specialist skills you have, although of course these often won't be as transferable to other employers unless you're staying in the same field.

Once your proof is as punchy as you can make it, the final writing task is to make everything as easy as possible for a busy recruiter.

The first person to read your CV may not have any job specific knowledge and they almost certainly won't have hours to spend poring over it. So it needs to be clear and to the point.

A clever summary which refers to the proof in your CV, coupled with a clearly expressed objective, will lead any reader neatly into the body of your CV – but even if time dictates that they stop there, at least they will have picked up all your most salient points.

Refining CVs

Again, many people would be tempted to stop after the writing stage. After all, you've thought up the proof of your skills, captured it, made it punchy and even produced a summary for the truly time-starved recruiter. Surely that's enough?

Well yes, it's enough to be able to technically call it a CV, but it's still in draft format. You've considered content, but not language or style. Language can be incredibly powerful so it's important you use the right words.

Verbs, or action words, are critical; if you don't use action words when describing yourself, then you won't come across as a person who acts to benefit their employer. Every basic action word belongs to a bigger family of action words, some of which hold more power than others. 'Made' is a basic action word that has similar, but more powerful, alternatives. People who 'invented', 'devised', 'created', 'built', sound more skilled than people who 'made' things, even if they are effectively doing the same thing. These power alternatives should be used to start your sentences and begin your bullet points.

There are also ways to communicate how good you are using adjectives, or description. Being concise in a CV is not the same as writing the bare minimum.

If you were part of a sales team, just putting 'member of the sales team' is certainly brief, but is it powerful? It's just a job description that hundreds of other salespeople could use. Including a word or two about what a great sales team it was will suddenly make you stand a foot taller than the 'ordinary' salespeople around you. Was it the league-winning, best-performing, highest-grossing, or most profitable sales team in the company? If it was, say so! If it wasn't, find an aspect of your performance that was extraordinary: you might not be the top salesperson in the company overall, but perhaps you've sold more of the latest model photocopier than anyone else.

Honesty

With such a strong focus on words, it can be rather tempting to just launch into a dictionary and round up the biggest and most impressive-sounding words you can. You might even feel it's okay to exaggerate or make a couple of things up, especially if it helps to conceal the areas you feel you are weak in.

It can't be stressed strongly enough that lying on a CV is not a good approach. There's no benefit to your CV as this should be focused on proof, not empty claims. If you get caught in a lie, the consequences are often fatal for your job prospects in that company.

Increasing numbers of employers are using pre-screening tests on applicants, because honesty is so important to them; employee fraud and dishonesty costs companies millions every year. When you lie on your CV it is more likely to prevent you getting an interview than to improve your chances.

Generally speaking, a false qualification or a fictional promotion adds less benefit to your CV than excellent writing throughout. What you can and should use, especially on what you may feel to be your problem areas, is an approach called honest spin.

Honest spin

Honest spin is about taking a positive view of every event or situation and no, it's not the same as blind optimism. Depending on your nature, the glass may be half empty or half full: either approach is absolutely fine. But spin is not about you, it's about the employer. What they want to know is that there is water in your glass, they can drink it, and that you are capable of getting more into it. What they don't need to know is how much you spilt when you tripped over.

When thinking about a potential problem on your CV, begin by writing your 'positive story'. This focuses on the good aspects of a problem area; for example, the skills you've developed while unemployed. It doesn't change the fact that you have not been working for a period of time, but it can switch the focus (and any discussion at interview) to what you've gained rather than what you may have lost.

Thinking about problem areas in advance is well worth doing: the right kind of spin can, even if unable to turn negatives into positives, at least distract attention from the main issue. Once you've refined your positive story and feel comfortable with it, it will also help you to talk as well as write more confidently.

Plain English

Concluding the section on refining language is jargon. Effectively a language all of its own with highly specialized speakers, jargon can be universal, industry-specific or company- and role-specific.

The basic guideline – in any context, not just CV writing – is that jargon should only be used when it adds to your audience's understanding. Mostly you don't know the audience for your CV: if it could confuse or raises doubt, leave it out. If you really can't leave it out, then ensure you explain it. This is particularly true if you come from a specialized background or are changing industry, or are moving from military to civilian employment.

Targeting CVs

With all the refining of language that's gone before, you may assume the writer's role is now over. If you were writing a novel, that might be a reasonable assumption. In actual fact for a CV you're still in full flow because the generic CV you've whittled and polished is now ready for its most important treatment: targeting. Once again, standing or sitting in the employers' shoes is essential.

While all of the previous processes add layer upon layer of value to your CV, targeting it to a specific role and a specific employer is possibly the most instantly noticeable. Targeting should never be forgotten. Yet there are plenty of people who do just that: who make multiple copies of their generic CV and send it out en masse for different job applications.

Doing this could waste all the time you've spent so far because targeting is the most effective tool for securing an interview.

Targeting means tapping into all your knowledge about a company, its marketplace and its activities. If you don't have much knowledge, make sure to top it up through research. You'll need this to create a positive story about why you fit so well with this particular employer and why you really want to work for them in this role.

The feeling that you're not being altogether genuine is a common one when you first begin targeting, but if your story is honest, well thought out and convincing then it can be a very powerful tool.

A recruiter who opens your envelope to see that you mention their company by name twice, have a long-standing passion for their products and have some valuable skills to contribute, is unlikely to dismiss your CV out of hand. This kind of flattery is potent. Who wouldn't want to employ someone who is genuinely keen to work for their company over someone who simply wants a job?

If you're serious about convincing an employer you're the one for them, think hard about convincing an employer that they're the one for you.

The process of targeting your CV can act as fantastic interview preparation: when you do get the good news, you'll already have answers in mind for many of the likely questions.

Targeting letters and other accompaniments

Your CV may be there to get you an interview, but your covering letter is there to get your CV read in the first place. As a result, it needs to draw from your targeted CV and be itself highly targeted, using the same language style and power techniques learned while CV writing to stand out from the pile of letters a recruiter will receive.

Being creative with your covering letter can be a good thing within the framework of the information you need to include. The structure isn't quite as formal as a CV which means you can include additional information that has no place on your CV. Quoting references or testimonials from previous employers can be a great way to demonstrate proof of your ability in a novel way. You can also mention relevant activities that may lie in the future – such as a course you have booked – to show how serious you are.

Your CV as part of your life

Writing your CV should never be considered a one-off event. When the deed is done and your powerful, effective, targeted CV has paid dividends in getting you interviews and job offers, don't just tuck your generic CV and this book away and forget all about them.

With relatively little effort your CV can be a living document, one that informs your choices and is informed by your actions. The benefits of keeping it alive are significant.

Every new skill example you perform (you'll notice more and more of these in your life once you've learned to pay attention to them) can be added to your generic CV and refined, building a bank of recent and powerful proof for which all the details are fresh in your memory.

On checking your CV and noticing it has stayed static for some months, you may be prompted to ask yourself the question – what more could I do to enhance it? Should I learn a new skill, take up a new interest, look for a new job with more challenges?

When the time comes that you really need your CV to be at its best – and quickly – it will need nothing more than targeting to create the impact you need.

Get started

While your life obviously influences your CV, your CV can also influence your life – in a positive way. For that reason, whether you need an amazing CV right now or just know you'll need one at some point in future, it's never too early to start building the framework.

1

How this book can help you

In this chapter you will:
- **understand the benefits of writing your own CV**
- **get started straight away**
- **decide where in the book to begin**

There are few guarantees in life, and employment is certainly not one of them. Despite hard work and careful choices, jobs can come and go quite unexpectedly.

The perfect opportunity that slipped by because you weren't quite ready for it; the too-good-to-be-true job offer that lived up to its name; that brilliant role ruined by a domineering manager with whom you simply couldn't get along; the seemingly secure job for life that disappeared just when you needed it most; the small gap in your employment that quickly expanded into a chasm.

Whether you welcome it or fear it, job searching is a part of almost everyone's life – now more than ever.

Competition for jobs

There is one thing you can guarantee when it comes to a job search: competition.

Most of us have had to fight to get the jobs we need and want; this was happening even before the catastrophic impact of the 2008 events on the global economy. If the company you work for goes under, it's not just you being left without a job. Tens or even hundreds of your co-workers will be in the same position. That raises the stakes: you're all chasing the same job opportunities at the same time.

Once the economy has started to stabilize, competition for jobs will probably keep rising because companies will remain very cautious about whom they take on.

Before the crash it wasn't uncommon to have 100 or more applicants chasing one vacancy – and that's not just the high flyers. However much or little experience you have, it's getting harder for anyone to reach interview stage.

Repeatedly being refused interviews, often with little or no explanation, can undermine anyone's self-confidence. If you were feeling a little shaky to start with, this can quickly become a problem. Before long you find yourself sending out applications that you don't really believe are going to get you anywhere. Once this happens, it's often clear to the person reading your application that you've given up. Unless you work for an anti-smoking charity, quitting is not a desirable quality in an employee.

What is a CV?

The one tool that everyone needs in a job search is a great CV, or Curriculum Vitae, which literally means 'the course of one's life'. Ignore the Latin roots: a CV is simply a brief written summary about you. It tells prospective employers three things:

- ▶ what you can do for their business
- ▶ why they should interview you for this job
- ▶ how to get in touch with you to arrange it.

You may hear it said that CVs are just for managers and professionals; this simply isn't true. From administrators to accountants, truck drivers to telesales reps, school leavers to shift workers, having a confident CV can only improve your chances of getting an interview for the job you want.

How can I write a CV?

Even if you don't feel your writing skill is anything to shout about yet, it will improve as this book takes you through every step of writing and refining your CV.

You're not alone if you find this daunting at first: many people find writing about themselves the hardest subject of all, one over which even the most confident communicator can stumble. It's easy to:

▶ believe your writing is not very good
▶ know what you want to say but struggle to find the right words
▶ think of so many 'good words' that the really important bits get overlooked
▶ just feel uncomfortable writing anything about yourself
▶ be unsure how to balance modesty with self-promotion
▶ have low confidence after being rejected for interviews
▶ not know what should be on your CV, or what it should look like
▶ wonder if you even need a CV anyway.

All these concerns will be addressed in this book.

The benefits of writing your own CV

Writing your own CV can take quite a bit of effort. But the rewards are worth it. Going through the process of preparing, writing and refining your own CV – and keeping it up to date – generates benefits at every stage of your job search.

This book can help you learn to:

- ▶ identify your skills and abilities
- ▶ deflect attention from your less positive aspects
- ▶ become comfortable writing – and talking – about yourself
- ▶ build your self-confidence
- ▶ see yourself from a prospective employer's viewpoint
- ▶ create a positive CV that you can still relate to
- ▶ write covering letters or fill out application forms
- ▶ refresh your memory before an interview
- ▶ highlight weaknesses you may wish to act upon
- ▶ ensure you are ready to act whenever an opportunity comes along.

A few of these benefits are discussed in more detail below.

Hard evidence

One great advantage of teaching yourself to write your own CV is that it becomes solid proof of your writing/communication skills.

Everyone needs to communicate at work. Most jobs involve some degree of writing, speaking, or both. Waiters pass orders to chefs, teachers write school reports, hauliers negotiate delivery slots with warehouses. Call centre operators soothe angry customers, senior managers justify a budget of millions and charity workers send out letters to potential donors. Every employer needs good communicators.

There's little point sending a badly written CV to try to convince an employer what a great communicator you are. They will just wonder what other skills you say you have, but actually don't. A clear, concise, well-written CV supports your claim to be a good communicator, because it provides proof. It *is* your proof.

CVs as personal trainers

Employers aren't the only ones who will benefit from your CV.
You can too. Try treating your CV as something you are doing
just for yourself.

You don't have to run marathons just because you start running
a mile every Wednesday. Improving your fitness is a good enough
reason to do it. Likewise, even if you don't have to send a CV when
applying for a job you can gain a lot by preparing one anyway.

With the help of this book, going through the process of writing
and refining your CV will help to develop the way you see yourself.
As you think more about what you can offer an employer, your
strengths will become clearer. The way you talk about yourself to
others will also become clearer.

That's the perfect state of mind to be in when searching for a job,
whether you are sending your first application or trying to impress
someone at final interview.

A personal CV

Employers don't receive piles of CVs that all *look* more or less the
same because employees all *are* more or less the same. They receive
stacks of them because most people don't spend enough time
preparing their CV, or don't know how.

Perhaps you sit or stand next to someone at work, in the classroom
or in the lecture theatre, who appears to do the same things you do,
with similar results. Your 'double'. Outwardly, they might seem
just as employable as you. If you both wanted the same job and
sent a CV, surely both of you (or neither of you) would get
interviewed?

Not necessarily. Despite obvious overlaps, you will each have skills that the other does not. Outside of work or study, other aspects of your lives won't be the same. How you write your CVs will also differ.

Like fingerprints, no two CVs should ever be identical. Whatever the surface similarities, every mix of skills, traits and experiences is individual. This uniqueness gradually becomes clear as you prepare, write and refine your own CV. Used well, it makes a good case for why you can do this job for this employer in a way that no one else can. This type of CV sees you invited for interview when your 'double' is not. In times of mass redundancy and layoffs, when you can find yourself on the market with dozens of similarly skilled people, this is crucial.

Cost-cutting CVs

Job searches often coincide with times when there isn't much money around. When you're on a budget, you can't get any cheaper than do-it-yourself.

Granted, there's the cost of this book. But how many reputable CV companies can offer a professionally written and tailored CV for the same price?

Of course, you could negotiate with the cheapest possible CV-writing company and save some cash that way. But beware, your name could end up at the top of a CV that – plus or minus a few tweaks – hundreds of other customers have already put their names to. There's no way of knowing whether an employer has already seen three other versions of the same CV when you add yours to the pile.

Writing a CV tailored for a client, for the job they want and for the employer they want to work for, takes considerable time to do properly. Time, unless it is your own, costs money. You'll only get as much of someone else's time and effort as you are prepared to pay for. Besides, you still need to make time to gather and provide all the content to the CV writer – work which, once done, sees you about a third of the way to a finished CV anyway.

Doing it yourself means you can then spend as much time on it as you wish to – you're not going to stop after four hours and tie up the loose ends because that's all you've been paid for. You can give yourself a CV by L'Oreal: Because you're worth it.

Just as importantly, when you learn to write your own CV you are gaining a valuable skill. Staying in the same job for the rest of your life is unlikely. You'll not only save money now, but every time you need to adapt your CV in future. Based on the old adage about fishing:

'Give a man a CV, and he can find a job.
Teach a man to write his own CV and he can be in control of his career.'

Realistic CV

The final benefit of writing your own CV is that, by the time you walk through the interview room door, you will be confident you can live up to this great CV.

No more worries about whether your CV makes you sound better than it should. No concerns about forgetting what it says, because you know it inside out; you wrote it. The words and phrases will be ones you feel comfortable using, can relate to, and suit your personality and way of speaking.

CVs that are written by someone else can often be overly high powered or formal. Saying 'extensive experience in a demanding customer service role' might not be appropriate if you have finished your A levels and are applying for your first office job. Especially if your only work experience is a bit of bar work on the odd evening since you sat your exams.

Even if this CV did get you the interview, it wouldn't help the interviewer build a very good picture of you. Chances are, they would feel that the person sitting in front of them is either faintly deluded or didn't write their own CV. Which raises the question in their mind, *why* didn't they write their own CV? Is there a weakness they need to try to uncover?

Phrasing the same section 'typical bar duties, serving customers and clearing tables' could, while more accurate, give the impression that the applicant lacks enthusiasm, skills, or both. Maybe this person felt they gained nothing from their experiences in this job.

A CV that says 'giving quick and cheerful service despite very long shifts, using humour and professionalism to defuse problems with drunken customers' would make a reader feel that they know a bit more about this applicant: their skills, and the kind of person they are. It's not so 'businessy' in style, but it is articulate and suggests a person you could rely on, who can solve problems, and who has the social skills to get on well with everyone in the office.

Which version would most make you want to interview the person for a job?

Getting the most out of this book

This book is split into sections that guide you through the various stages of creating your own CV. Throughout there are plenty of practical examples to show how different ways of saying the same thing can create different impressions. These examples are designed to help you develop your CV writing skills, build your confidence and avoid making common mistakes.

Example

Good

2002–2004 Customer Relations Adviser, CVS Assurance
▶ Handling customer complaints and queries by phone.

Better

2002–2004 Customer Relations Adviser, CVS Assurance
▶ Handling customer service complaints as part of a busy team, logging and directing calls appropriately to meet monthly service targets.

Best

2002–2004 Customer Relations Adviser, CVS Assurance
▶ Working with other departments to sort out more than 30 customer complaints a day.
▶ One of only two team members to exceed 97% customer satisfaction target.

Where to start

You can start with page one and work through the book in order, or use it as a reference guide and just jump in. Each section stands alone: if at any stage you think you've missed an important point, just flick back a chapter or two.

Sections:
Part one: Preparing the details
Part two: Writing the basics
Part three: Refining your language
Part four: Targeting it carefully
Part five: Presenting it perfectly
Part six: Using it properly

Parts one and two: Preparing the details and Writing the basics
You're writing your first CV, want a basic refresher or need to start again from scratch.

Part three: Refining your language
Your draft CV is written but you're not happy with how it sounds.

Part four: Targeting it carefully
You're confident your CV content and style is good, but still no interviews.

Part five: Presenting it perfectly
Your CV content is well targeted, but it looks cramped and key points are hard to find.

Part six: Using it properly
Your CV is finished and you want to get as much as you can out of it.

By the time you finish this book, you will hopefully:

▶ have used skills you didn't know you had, or developed new ones
▶ be able to see yourself in a new and positive light
▶ feel delighted with the confident CV you have prepared.

What about using a professional CV writer?

It is possible that, after following every step and with feedback from friends and colleagues, you still feel you can't do yourself justice. In that case, if you have the money, a professional CV writing company could be the right next step for you.

If you do decide to use a professional CV company, please don't view this process as a waste of your time. Every stage ferrets out relevant details about yourself and your skills. These details not only help prepare you for interviews, but any good CV writer will hug you – in a professional way of course – for providing them. The old computer maxim 'garbage in, garbage out' definitely applies to professional CV writing: the better thought out the information you provide, the higher quality CV you'll get.

However you go about obtaining a CV you are comfortable and happy with – whether you write it yourself or have it written for you – the sections on targeting, presenting and using your CV properly are still very valuable.

Take your time

There are no shortcuts to writing a confident, persuasive CV. Whichever route you choose to get to first draft stage, self-written or professionally written, you still need to give yourself time to think about it in depth.

Rewriting your CV for each job you apply for will take even more time – unless you're prepared to spend plenty of money having someone do all the targeting for you.

It's not melodramatic to say that your CV is a powerful, life-changing tool. Getting the job you need or want – or not getting it – has a huge impact on your lifestyle and wellbeing.

Many people spend more time and effort applying for their mortgage than they do applying for their job. Yes, buying a house is a huge commitment – but as you end up spending more of your waking time at work than at home anyway, why is so little time spent on a CV? Especially as it's the work that pays the mortgage!

Passing the buck is not an option. Yes, the odd person gets away with it but it's not a great strategy for getting an interview or a job. Like it or not, you will need to spend time on your CV if it is to get the results you are after.

When should I start my CV?

Now! It's never too early. Unless perhaps you are at primary school, in which case you can cut yourself a little slack for a few years.

It doesn't matter whether you are preparing for exams at school, college or university or have just changed job. Perhaps you are starting maternity leave soon, waiting for redundancy or looking for the next career move. Preparing or refining your CV before it becomes urgent has many advantages. You:

- ▶ avoid that last-minute scrabble for details you might have lost
- ▶ remember the most important elements from each stage of your life
- ▶ collect examples of your skills before babies appear and steal them (which they do)
- ▶ think about yourself as an employable person while you are still employed (frame of mind can be very important)
- ▶ don't miss out on sudden opportunities

- ▶ respond quickly and calmly to every vacancy
- ▶ focus on refining your CV instead of panicking
- ▶ use it as a memory aid for application forms and interviews
- ▶ start thinking about ways you can enhance your employability.

Don't put it off, even if you feel a bit daunted at the thought of writing a CV. Even if you think it's not a priority because you're a bit pushed for time. It's far better to start now, than when your need for a job becomes urgent and the pressure is on.

Giving yourself time and space to think about your CV in stages, coming back to it when you feel inspired, will create a better and more considered result.

Even when you're not thinking about a career change, writing your CV might inspire a fresh job search – maybe in a different direction.

That's more than enough reasons to get on with writing your CV. You're ready to start.

TEN THINGS TO REMEMBER

1 *Job hunting is a competition.*

2 *Your CV must stand out and show you offer something different.*

3 *Everyone can improve their CV using language and layout.*

4 *Be prepared to invest time in creating a great CV.*

5 *Always think about yourself in a positive way.*

6 *Write your own CV to prove you have communication skills.*

7 *Learning to write your own CV helps prepare you for interviews.*

8 *Always have your CV ready before you really need it.*

9 *Using a CV writer doesn't mean doing nothing yourself.*

10 *It's never too early to start writing your CV: why not today?*

Part one

Preparing the details

This stage is a bit like a treasure hunt. All you need to do is remember – or dig out – the right details and put them all down in one place.

Preparation is a purely factual process: there's no wordsmithing needed. All that's required is total honesty, so that you get a complete and accurate picture of yourself.

Gaps in your work history or other problems are fine; they will be sorted out later.

So there's no excuse not to start straight away ...

2

Getting the basic details together

In this chapter you will learn how to:
- *pull together accurate facts about yourself, your skills and your experience*
- *understand what to put in and what to leave out*

The following headings cover the key pieces of information you will need to write down, check or think about in this section:

- ▶ Personal details: name, address, telephone number, email.
- ▶ Your personal information: discrimination law, disability, security.
- ▶ Education: accuracy and proof.
- ▶ Career, employment or work history: company details, first jobs, voluntary work.
- ▶ Professional qualifications and memberships.
- ▶ Further skills and training.
- ▶ Interests.
- ▶ References: professional and personal.

Personal details

NAME

Your CV should start with your name. Don't put 'Curriculum Vitae' or 'CV' at the top, because everyone knows what they're looking at. You don't write 'Shopping List' above a list of bread, milk, beans and toilet roll; your CV doesn't need to be labelled either.

The name you put doesn't have to be the full one from your birth certificate. Roger Winston Richard Johnson can just be Roger Johnson. If your first name is Christopher but everyone calls you Chris, put Chris. For a first name that is unusual, long, or often mispronounced, you might feel more comfortable using a shortened or anglicized version. This could be the name friends or colleagues normally call you.

Harichou could become Hari or Harry, Abhayankari might change to Abha or Abby, or Gbone turns to Bonnie. When doing this, be careful not to end up sounding like a nickname or a joke. Shortening Madi any further could give the wrong impression. It's better to wait until the interview to admit that your colleagues call you Mad!

In general, if you're not a native speaker of the language in which you have to write your CV, or a resident of the country in which you're applying for a job, it's a good idea to check name changes (as a minimum) with someone who is.

Insight

Abbreviating names can change gender. This shouldn't affect your chances of interview but can cause confusion! Christine shortened to Chris might imply a male: changing Madhusudhana to Madi might imply a female. If you prefer your gender clear – it doesn't have to be – you can always add a Miss, Ms, Mrs or Mr to your CV and covering letter.

CONTACT DETAILS

Standard practice is to list your:

▶ home address
▶ telephone number
▶ email address.

Address
State your full postal address, including an accurate postcode.

Telephone number
Be sure to include the area code and double check it is correct. Most recruiters will bin a CV if they dial the contact number and the person who answers has never heard of you.

For landlines, be clear which number you have given: work or home. The recruiter is less likely to leave an urgent message on a home number or expect you to call back the same day.

By including a work number, be prepared for calls at work. If you can't talk in front of others and no one knows you are considering leaving, it's best not to give this. Also, if you're sending your CV to a lot of places, you might get a lot of calls – which could tax the patience of the most understanding employer.

Try to stick to just one number if you can – it's far simpler and quicker for the person trying to contact you if there is only one option.

Mobile numbers are usually the best, as long as you have a signal during the day. If not, home numbers are better than work, but make sure your answering machine or voicemail works properly or your family know to take a message carefully. Getting home to find you've been invited to interview but no one can tell you when, or with whom, would be very frustrating. Be sure to check voicemail messages regularly.

Insight
Don't forget your own answerphone message. It can speak volumes about you. 'Hi, it's us, we're either too drunk or too stoned to get to the phone right now but if you leave your number we'll get back to you ... one day ...' might entertain your friends but employers won't feel quite so excited about inviting you for interview.

If you will be sending your CV overseas, add the relevant international dialling code for your country. If you're not certain what that is, check online or in your phone directory. The code for dialling to the UK from abroad is +44.

The typical way to write your number internationally is the country dialling code first, then the zero at the start of your UK number in brackets as it is left out:

- ▶ 01234 567 891 turns into +44 (0)1234 567 891
- ▶ 07777 123 456 becomes +44 (0)7777 123 456

Email
Choose your email address with care.

Will an employer cheer inwardly at the thought of employing facebookaddict@yahoo.co.uk, popmycherry@hotmail.com, thevodkamaster@googlemail.com or imabigloser@virgin.net?

However amusing the story behind your online ID, at best they'll be unimpressed and at worst put off from even reading your CV. Facebookaddict suggests a person more likely to spend their time social networking than working, while imabigloser won't necessarily make them think you've been on a successful weight loss programme.

If in any doubt, or you don't have an email address yet, it's easy to set up a free email account and choose a more professional-sounding address.

Try to keep your name the central focus of the address, even if you do have to include some numbers, and make it as simple as possible. anthonyperfect09@hotmail.com is infinitely better than 18756ii901lghif@hotmail.com: it's instantly clear who it belongs to, is less likely to be entered incorrectly, and probably won't be automatically classed as spam when you reply to a message.

Email addresses need to be as carefully checked as contact numbers when you type them. One letter or number out of place and your invitation to an interview will end up in someone else's inbox or lost forever in webspace. No recruiter or employer will try ten different versions of your email address to see if they land on the right one.

Insight

Check your email address doesn't automatically become a hyperlink (coloured and underlined) when entered into your electronic CV. If it does, the colour can be hard to read or lost completely when it is printed or photocopied. Reformat it by highlighting, removing the underline and changing the font colour back to black or, if in Microsoft Word, just right-click on the link and select 'Remove Hyperlink'.

Personal information

Anti-discrimination law means you do NOT need to put your:

▶ age or date of birth
▶ state of health
▶ gender
▶ race
▶ marital status
▶ sexual orientation
▶ number of dependants
▶ religious beliefs
▶ any other personal information

on your CV.

Legal stuff aside, this kind of detail doesn't tell an employer anything useful anyway. Your focus should only be what you can offer them, and how well you can do the job.

There's no point in being too precious about this though, because some details are going to become clear as they read through your CV:

▶ Your name may point to your gender.
▶ The level of education you've completed and the date you started your first job will indicate your likely age.
▶ Attending a faith school might hint at your religious beliefs.
▶ Maternity leave in your work history strongly suggests you are female, and that you have at least one child. As for paternity leave – well, it's not rocket science!

However, none of this information needs to be volunteered, nor is it relevant. If you mention that you are a widower with 17 children, some human resources departments may delete these details before forwarding your CV internally, so that discrimination cannot play any part. If not, then at best you have wasted CV space on information that is not relevant to your ability to do a job. At worst, you could raise a query in the interviewer's mind whether a man with 17 children to raise alone might prioritize family over work.

Insight

You may be asked to provide personal details such as gender, ethnicity, age, etc., on a separate form or while filling out an online application. Do provide it in the format requested, never on your CV. This information can legally be requested and used by employers to track Equal Opportunities performance, not to influence recruitment.

DISABILITY

Health and disability can be a grey area.

You are under no obligation to mention any disability or health problems when applying for a job. However, you could disadvantage yourself if you don't. This is especially true if you need support to get your application in, or to access an interview.

Employers must provide reasonable support so anyone can compete for one of their jobs on an equal basis. Depending on your disability or illness, it could be worthwhile revealing relevant details in advance and requesting any specific help you may need. Even if you don't include it in your CV, you can say so in your covering letter.

Turning up for interview in a wheelchair that you didn't mention in your application can mean awkwardness all round if, for example, you can't access the interview room being used. The interviewer may, quite rightly, wonder why on earth you didn't say something sooner so that other arrangements could have been made for you.

On the other hand, if your disability or ill health is less obvious, you may decide – and successfully manage – to keep it hidden throughout the recruitment process.

Employers are allowed to ask candidates if they have a disability that might affect their ability to do the job they have applied for. But the employer also has to make any reasonable changes to the workplace that are needed for a disabled person to do the job as effectively as anyone else. This could be something quite simple, like providing a special screen for a computer so that a sight-impaired person can read it clearly, or suitable office equipment for someone who suffers from back problems.

If you wish to keep your disability or ill health hidden, then that is your legal right. You are not obliged to admit or volunteer any information, even when asked directly. However, if your disability stops you from doing your job adequately at some point in the future, and you face losing your job, you can't fall back on the Disability Discrimination Act. This Act only protects those who actually tell an employer about their disability or ill health. If this issue affects you, it is worth getting further advice.

SECURITY

From a personal security standpoint, it is not a good idea to send out any documents that contain your name, address, phone number *and* date of birth. This information alone is often enough for someone to commit identity fraud.

Literally hundreds of people could have access to the information in your CV. Before you are tempted to 'pad' your CV with irrelevant details to make it look longer and more impressive, think carefully about the security implications – if not the style.

Unless you are asked to provide proof of UK residence with an application, such as a National Insurance number or your Passport number, never offer it on your CV. Normally, it's enough to confirm you are a UK resident. Later in the recruitment process is when you might reasonably be asked to provide proof. Even if this proof is requested at the same time as your CV, you can send it in a separate letter or try phoning with the details.

Insight

Be careful what you put on your CV. It can end up in more places than you might imagine:

▶ every employer you've applied to directly
▶ recruitment agencies you've contacted
▶ every employer an agency has sent your CV to
▶ unrelated people, when accidentally forwarded with an email
▶ every job-hunting website and CV library you approached.

Your CV may hang around for a long time. When it's no longer needed, you can't be sure it will be deleted or lovingly shredded.

Education

This step can be a bit disheartening if you are not overly proud of your education. Don't worry – if it isn't a star, it doesn't have to take centre stage.

First, ensure all your facts are correct. Find the original certificates and:

- ▶ Note down where you studied and when, including all the subjects, levels and grades.
- ▶ Include all your academic studies: GCSE, O Level, CSE, Standard, AS Level, A Level, Higher, BTEC, NVQ, City & Guilds, Baccalaureate, Bachelor's degree, Master's degree, PhD, etc.
- ▶ If you have studied beyond GCSE level (or CSE/O Levels), list your education in reverse date order: the highest level (i.e. most recent) education at the top of the list.
- ▶ Put the certificates together, labelled, where you can easily find them again.

It might seem like overkill to dig out original certificates, but there are two good reasons:

1 ACCURACY

Even if your student years are not a distant memory, it's worth being sure that what you put down is 100 per cent correct. This is very important if you've been guilty of exaggeration on past CVs. Say something often enough and you can start to believe it yourself.

Lies of any kind on a CV are a bad idea, and will be discussed in more detail in Chapter 7. Even if you aren't convinced the truth could ever be made to look good, go through this stage anyway. You're the only person who will see this information in this format.

2 PROOF

Any employer can ask for evidence of your qualifications, and at any time. Being unable to produce them can be embarrassing and frustrating, especially if your job offer relies on this proof. Getting copies can take a long time, assuming it's even possible.

Recent school leavers and graduates should have an advantage: hopefully you know where your certificates are. Make sure you can find them again whenever you need them. You might be surprised how far into the future your results will be checked, as it often depends on company policy. It's not unknown for an employer to request a degree certificate ten years or more after it was awarded.

With your education accurately recorded, you can start shaping it into something positive. Details can be expanded, shortened or deleted once you start to refine your CV.

But for now, it's enough just to have it all in one place.

Career, employment or work history

What you call this section depends on your viewpoint. After spending ten years in warehousing and distribution to become a logistics manager, or working your way up from kitchen hand to assistant head chef, 'Career History' works fine.

If you haven't been working long, or have jumped around from personal trainer to delivery driver to cruise ship entertainer, it's harder to say you've followed a career. 'Employment History' or 'Work History' might be more apt. It's really a matter of what you feel most comfortable with. Any of these titles makes it clear to the reader of your CV what they'll find in this section.

List whom you've worked for in a paid capacity: what role, when and for how long.

Just like Education, this section should be in reverse date order with your current or most recent job at the top.

DESCRIBE THE COMPANY

If you've worked for a company that isn't well known, their name might not mean anything to the person reading your CV. Working as a manager for Megabucks for five years says nothing useful about you on its own.

But, when you add that Megabucks was:

▶ a new, fast-growing UK chain of coffee outlets, or
▶ a well-established family business importing moose hides from Canada, or
▶ a global manufacturer of high-tech money-printing machines

then the reader gets an instant picture. All of a sudden they can imagine the kind of business environment you've worked in, even if they've never heard of the company.

If you're not sure how best to describe an employer, the 'About Us' section of their website is good for ideas. Try to keep the description to one line or so, and include these key details:

▶ industry: e.g. retail, importer, manufacturer
▶ products/services: e.g. coffee, moose hides, money-printing machines
▶ size: national, family, global
▶ status: established, new, market-leading, fast-growing, high tech, etc.

If you've been a temp and employed by many firms for short periods, or a contractor working on one project after another, or a manager who has moved companies many times during a 20-year career, your employment list could end up quite long. When you come to refine this section, you may group or even omit certain jobs if they are old or irrelevant to the position you are applying for.

As you never know which direction the future will take, put it all in for now.

Your first job

School leavers and graduates are unlikely to have much to write here compared to someone who has worked for years, but this doesn't make any work experience less valid. You might want to avoid calling it your Career History though. Paid holiday roles, job shadowing and work experience are often better put under Work History or Work Experience.

Most schools encourage work experience, so don't forget to include everything you've done, even if it was just for a few days. Compared to school leavers and graduates with no work experience, you'll look more interesting.

Voluntary work

Just because it's unpaid doesn't mean it's unskilled or useless by any means.

Voluntary work is not a poor cousin of paid work – it often uses many of the same skills, so don't be tempted to sweep it under the carpet. List any voluntary work you have done here, although for ease keep it in a separate section to your paid work.

You may decide to take it out later, or leave it in your CV if it's relevant to a job you want to apply for. Part-time voluntary work in an animal shelter could be great to mention if you decide you want to become a veterinary nurse or work as a fundraising manager for an animal charity.

Finding work after being made redundant can take time. Being unemployed leaves a gap in your CV that will at some point need to be explained – and the bigger the gap, the longer the explanation. If it's at all likely that when you finish one job the next one could take a while to appear, it might be worth seeing if there's any voluntary work you could do. The same applies if you've already been unemployed for a while, and claiming benefits doesn't stop you from doing voluntary work if you follow the rules. While making applications and going to interviews, voluntary work can keep you in the habit of doing regular work as well as helping to close the CV 'gap'.

If the voluntary work you have done is occasional rather than regular, you might prefer to include it in the Interests section instead.

Write what you did

Once you have your list of dates, companies and job titles, note exactly what you did in each job. Again it's pure information you want at this stage, not something you'll present in a finished CV. Jot down as much as you can remember, without trying to work out whether or not it sounds impressive. You can refine it later.

Your current or most recent job should be the easiest, so it's often best to start with that. If you get stuck, or can't think how to describe what you did, try answering a few of the questions below. Many job responsibilities involve working with one or more of the following:

- ▶ people
- ▶ money/finance
- ▶ systems
- ▶ thinking
- ▶ training/learning.

Even if you're not stuck, these job responsibilities all require general skills that most employers are interested in, so they're a useful way to think about what you've done.

PEOPLE

Does your job involve dealing with people?

If so:

- ▶ Do you do it in person, by phone or in writing (letter/email)?
- ▶ Are these people from your own company or other companies? From the media? Customers or members of the public?
- ▶ Do you serve or help these people, work with them as part of a team, negotiate with them, or manage them?

Most jobs involve dealing with people in some way – from bar staff to horse riding instructors, from marketing managers for global corporations to doctor's receptionists.

You might treat patients, work in customer service, carry out market research, manage your own business, sell life insurance, fix computers, handle billing queries in a call centre, arrange events, pick and pack orders in a warehouse or work as a personal assistant. All these activities need good people skills.

Try to mention:

- ▶ how often you dealt with people
- ▶ how many you dealt with
- ▶ who they were
- ▶ how you dealt with them.

MONEY/FINANCE

Do you deal with money in any way?

This could be:

- ▶ handling cash and/or credit card payments, cashing up
- ▶ bookkeeping, creating invoices
- ▶ selling goods and services, negotiating prices

- paying staff
- buying goods or services in from suppliers
- planning or managing a budget
- working out ways to save money or increase profits
- fundraising.

Many types of work give you some level of responsibility for money, or for profitability.

Try to ensure you mention anything that could show the kind of skills you have.

Working in a bar or shop often means handling cash and credit card payments, maybe even cashing up at the end of the day. Perhaps you carry the takings to the bank. Any of this could suggest you are good with numbers, careful and, above all, trustworthy.

Maybe you buy stationery for an office and shop around for the best deal so you don't overspend. Or perhaps you organized a Christmas party for your team at work and got a discount from a local restaurant so everyone could afford to go. This kind of activity suggests you are comfortable with numbers, can plan well, can manage a budget and can negotiate.

Any aspect of a job that includes money or finance is worth recording.

SYSTEMS

Do you use a system? Not just computers, but any kind of system:

- email, internet, intranet, or other office software/systems
- electronic tills, filing systems, stock control systems
- logistics, distribution tracking, warehousing systems
- accounts, invoicing, financial reporting, expenses, payroll, SAP
- planning, forecasting, ordering, project management systems
- design, engineering, CAD, print, manufacturing, etc.

It doesn't really matter which type of system you may use, the key thing is that you can learn and successfully use a system – and could learn to use a new system if needed, for a new employer.

Be sure to note down:

- ▶ how many/which systems you use
- ▶ whether the systems are universal or specific to this company
- ▶ how often you use it/them
- ▶ whether you help or train other people to use it/them.

THINKING SKILLS

How much thought, judgement or decision making does your job need to be done well?

For example, do you:

- ▶ solve problems for yourself, or colleagues or customers at work?
- ▶ come up with new ideas or design new things?
- ▶ think up simpler, faster, better or more efficient ways to do something?
- ▶ have to make decisions or judgements whilst at work?

For example, a truck driver plans his route each morning. He aims to use as little fuel as possible and to pass filling stations with cheap diesel. However, he also makes last-minute changes to avoid traffic delays so that every delivery window is met. This means he is showing good thinking and decision-making skills, which all employers find useful.

The paint factory worker who suggests a change to the production line to prevent so many tins being damaged and thrown away is showing good problem-solving skills.

A flight attendant or bar manager who watches customers' drinking habits and behaviour carefully so that he can decide when to stop serving – or, assuming the bar is not airborne at the time, when to ask them to leave – is using good judgement.

TRAINING/LEARNING

As well as doing your job, do you ever help or train other people?

This doesn't mean you have to be an official 'training manager', or even have 'training' in your job description. It might be something you do just because you are experienced, or because people are always asking you for help.

You could be the person who shows the factory machines to new staff and temps. Or the one who explains the office filing system or how to claim expenses. Maybe you run a Health & Safety induction course for all new employees.

Think about the following:

▶ Do you teach or demonstrate anything to anyone?
▶ Are you the one always showing new staff how the filing system works?
▶ Once you've fixed something, do you then explain to someone how to prevent it from breaking again?
▶ Do you mentor or coach someone in a more junior role?
▶ Do you give presentations teaching other colleagues about what you do?

Whether a dedicated training manager or informal trainer or coach, try to note down:

▶ how many people you train or coach
▶ how often you train them
▶ who they are/what level i.e. colleagues/customers, juniors/peers/senior managers
▶ what you teach them
▶ why you are the person chosen/who volunteers to do it.

Professional qualifications and memberships

List the type, level and date of professional qualifications. Also, put the date and level of memberships of relevant organizations. For example:

▶ Member of the Chartered Management Institute since 2007
▶ 1995 – Member of the Royal Veterinary College
▶ 2009 Graduate Member of the Institute of Export (Associate Member since 2006)
▶ Student Member of the Institute of Civil Engineers (2008)

If you do not yet hold a relevant professional qualification but are working towards one, and are able to become a student or associate member, it may help to show a recruiter that you are serious about a career in the industry.

Further skills and training

This section covers qualifications or training courses that don't fall into the Education or Employment sections of your CV. What you call this depends on what you can include.

You might have taken further professional qualifications, specializing in a certain area or adding to your skills. These could be listed under 'Professional Development', for example:

▶ Microsoft or Cisco accreditation
▶ Quality Systems training
▶ Project Management qualifications.

Other recognized qualifications gained through external examinations can also be covered here, perhaps under a heading such as 'Further Skills':

▶ Secretarial: RSA Typing Level I and II, Pitman Shorthand
▶ Language: Chamber of Commerce French for Business, Certificado Inicial in Spanish as a Foreign Language
▶ Driving: HGV licence, Forklift licence
▶ IT: CLAIT (Computer Literacy And Information Technology)
▶ Culinary: Cordon Bleu
▶ Other: First Aid At Work, Food Hygiene, Nursery/ Childcare, etc.

For all the above recognized qualifications you may need to provide proof that you have attained an accepted level of expertise in that subject or field, so find any certificates now. Check also that your certificates are current and not lapsed.

Other training courses could be specific to your employer or industry:

▶ In-house systems: company-specific ordering, stock control, project management, expense, manufacturing, creative, monitoring and internal systems, platforms and databases, etc.
▶ Software: Microsoft Word, Excel, PowerPoint and Access; Adobe Photoshop, SAP, Oracle, Sage Line 50, company-specific packages, etc.
▶ Programming skills: Visual Basic, C++, Java, etc.
▶ Sales: professional selling skills, product training, negotiation skills, presentation skills, etc.
▶ Management: effective management, leadership skills, etc.
▶ Other: diversity/cultural training, disability awareness, health and safety.

How much you include in your final CV depends on how relevant it is: but at this stage try to write everything down.

Interests

Not everyone likes to include this section on their CV – and sometimes there may be good reasons not to – but for this initial step, note it all so it is not forgotten.

By the end of the CV-refining step you might find that some of the skills you learned while pursuing your interests could be quite valuable and perhaps appealing to an employer.

Things you can include in this section are:

- ▶ sports you teach, play or regularly support
- ▶ non-sporting clubs or teams you may be a member of: this could be the local carnival committee, film club, pub quiz team, history club, etc.
- ▶ other activities you enjoy regularly: street dance, quiz nights, skateboarding, off-road driving, stand-up comedy, theatre productions, barber shop group, learning to play an instrument, cookery lessons, etc.
- ▶ charity, community or voluntary work: fundraising event for a hospice, helping with a scout camp, reading to a blind friend, urban community project, hospital visiting, etc. This may take a more prominent position in your work history if you are currently out of work or are a school leaver with no other work experience.
- ▶ hobbies: tracing family history, restoring old cars, showing pedigree poodles, wildlife photography, silk painting, cake decorating, short story competitions, etc.

Generally speaking this list should be quite brief, although if you go beyond 'standard' participation and do anything at a higher level it is worth saying so. If you hold a position of responsibility within a club or team (i.e. you are Treasurer, Membership Secretary, Editor, Chairman, etc.) then put that down.

If you have passed exams, won awards recently or had other successes, mention them too – although do keep it all recent.

If you can, date it now – when you come back to this list in a year or two it might not be so easy to remember what you did and when.

A long list at this point is not a problem: you will edit this down during the writing and refining stages.

Harder to address is the opposite: if your list feels a bit short or unimpressive and you don't have much to say in other parts of your CV either (because you are a recent school leaver or graduate), don't panic. And whatever you do, don't try to pad it out by making something up.

Falsely claiming to be a keen skydiver gets you rumbled when your interviewer (or their sister/best friend/husband/wife/son) happens to be an extreme sports fanatic and you can't name a single drop zone you've jumped. Assuming you got through the interview unscathed, your reputation would definitely suffer when you refuse to join the office's annual charity parachute jump.

If you don't like the way your interests section looks now, bear in mind you can always take up a new interest whenever you want. It doesn't have to cost money, and you might learn one or more potentially useful skills.

The Interests section may be seen by some employers and candidates as the least important part of your CV, but it is also one of the easiest areas to change – and quickly. It's what you make of it that matters: you can always leave it out of your finished CV if it doesn't add anything.

References

These generally aren't needed up front, but it's worth sorting out the details now.

Typically you need one professional and one personal reference, although this may vary depending on the role and industry.

The professional one tends to come from a former employer (ideally the most recent), while the personal one can come from anyone who knows you well.

It pays to check in advance that someone is happy to be a referee for you, not least because you need to be sure that what they will say about you is appropriate – and positive. Being a referee can also take up quite a bit of time. You might apply for roles in several organizations and find that all want to see references before you receive any provisional job offers. When this happens, your referees may find themselves filling out lots of forms in a short space of time, and some can be very detailed.

PROFESSIONAL REFEREES

If you have a great working relationship with your current manager (and the feeling is mutual), and you move jobs, it's worth asking if they would be prepared to do one or both of these things:

1 Be a referee that prospective employers can contact in future.
2 Provide a general written reference that highlights your key strengths/skills.

Both types of reference can be very useful; while prospective employers often want to ask specific questions on a set form about your capabilities and history, a standard reference can also be useful. There are three great advantages of a standard reference:

▸ it is written when you are still fresh in that person's mind
▸ it can act as a great aid for you when writing future CVs/ applications
▸ you know in advance exactly what it says.

Of course if you do ask your manager to be a referee, ask for their personal contact details in case they too move job before you need their input. It's all very well having a great professional referee, but only if you can actually track them down when you need them.

PERSONAL REFEREES

Many people struggle a bit more when it comes to their personal references.

Can you put down your mum? You could in theory, if the employer has not specified no relatives, but that's not to say you should. Your mother's opinion will probably not be given nearly as much weight as an unrelated referee, so using her could work against you.

Generally speaking, using any close family is a bit of a no-no, unless of course you have worked for or with them in a family business.

Assuming that because your sister has married and has a different surname no one will know you are related, can be a mistake. Question one for a personal referee is usually something like: 'How long have you known Fred, and in what capacity?' It's a bad idea to lie, and it's even worse asking someone else to do it for you.

Personal references are best coming from a friend who has known you for a long time. A work colleague that you are friendly with, or have worked with for many years, may also have particularly good insight into your qualities.

If you're a school leaver or student and your own friends aren't employed yet, you may be better off asking a family friend to be your reference, unless you trust your friends to take this duty as seriously as they need to. If you ask a boyfriend or girlfriend to be your referee, bear in mind what might happen if you split up before they have finished this task. Bitter exes do not generally give great feedback about their former loves.

Friends who work in a similar field or position to the one you want may have a better feel for what a prospective employer will want to know, and how to cast you in a positive light.

USING YOUR REFEREES

Your referees will thank you for making their job easy. Be sure to explain, before your referees get asked about you, which job/s you've applied for, and what skills and abilities they seem to be looking for. Remind them how you think you fit the bill.

There are several ways you can use references, from quoting standard letters to including appraisal comments or copying sections of congratulatory emails. If you have any positive written feedback or recognition from any of your past employers, managers or colleagues, then keep it safe.

There is more on the creative use of references in Part six, Using it properly.

Beware!

Employers have a lot to lose by employing dishonest employees. Fraud costs UK companies millions of pounds every day, and much of it is committed by employees, or with inside help. It's not hard to see why vetting new employees is something many take seriously.

Some employers don't just screen applicants; they may also screen potential employees' references. They may check things like how long your referee has lived at their current or previous address, whether they have any convictions, county court judgments or bankruptcies on record. Attempts may also be made to double check whether you have any known connections with them.

Ensure that any references you do provide will stand up to scrutiny, warn your referees before they are contacted, and thank them afterwards.

TEN THINGS TO REMEMBER

1 *Good preparation makes CV writing quicker and easier.*

2 *Always keep certificates and other proof where you can find them.*

3 *Build up a picture of your experience and skills.*

4 *Think about what you actually do at work, not what your job title says.*

5 *This is your private factsheet: time to be totally honest, warts and all.*

6 *Don't include irrelevant personal details.*

7 *Choose whether or not to mention any disabilities – if in doubt, get advice.*

8 *Once you send out your CV, you can't control who sees it or where it goes.*

9 *Choose your references carefully and ask their permission.*

10 *Employers may use a security company to screen applicants.*

Part two

Writing the basics

Good news – you now have all the basic information for the different sections of your CV. A factsheet, if you like. It probably looks a bit like a CV already, but it's not ready to send yet. This chapter is where the actual writing begins.

If everyone stopped at factsheet stage (and many do), there would be hundreds if not thousands of similar-sounding CVs out there for anyone who does a similar job. How lucky would you have to be for an employer to choose yours from that pile?

Take the first step towards getting your CV chosen. Transform your basic employment facts (who you worked for and in what position) into a description of you: what you've done, what you are capable of and what you have to offer a future employer. This may seem like quite a task, and it is.

Part two will require quite a lot of thought. It will help you to think differently about yourself and what you have done. Of all the stages of CV writing, this should be one of the longest – but it becomes much easier when you break it down into chunks.

3

....

What skills do you have?

In this chapter you will learn how to:
- *understand what employers want to hear*
- *tell them how good you are*
- *prove what you say*

What makes you attractive?

The answer has nothing to do with physical appearance. How attractive you are to an employer is based purely on what you can offer them.

What you have done in the past will give most employers the best indication of what you can offer them in future. Their initial focus is most likely to be your Employment section.

Make it personal

An ideal Employment section is a series of bullet points in which you show off your skills.

What it is not, is a simple list of job responsibilities.

A list of job duties won't make you stand out from anyone else who does a similar job. Employers don't want to know what you were supposed to be doing in another job; they want to know what you actually did in that job, and what you can therefore do for them.

Prove yourself

The key to doing this well is proof. Each bullet point must give some evidence that supports your claim to have these skills.

When you think about it, anyone can claim to be anything. We can all claim to be amazingly motivated, valuable, committed, skilled employees. If all you do is make claims, there's no reason for a recruiter to believe you. And no way to tell you apart from others.

The moment you start coming up with examples to show that what you say is true, your CV starts to gather real power.

Building your Employment section

Starting with your most recent job in mind, try to answer the following three questions:

1 *WHAT DID YOU ACTUALLY DO?*

Don't rely too much on your job title to explain your past roles. What your job title says you do in your current company is often not the same at other companies you apply to.

Question: Which of these is the most senior sales position?

▶ Territory Sales Manager
▶ Regional Sales Executive
▶ Regional Account Manager
▶ Sales Development Executive
▶ Regional Sales Manager
▶ New Business Executive
▶ National Account Manager
▶ Customer Development Manager

Answer: It depends. Even where the same title is used, the levels of responsibility can vary enormously. One company's office manager can be another's post sorter and coffee maker.

Accurately note what you did/do for each company you've worked for, and at what level.

From the following list, note what you were/are handling:

▶ workload
▶ team sizes
▶ team complexity
▶ project deadlines
▶ budget sizes
▶ performance targets.

Specific detail is what will make it clear to another employer whether you are likely to be able to cope with the level of job you are applying for.

2 HOW WELL DID YOU DO WHAT YOU DID?

A CV that gives only a list of your job responsibilities doesn't say whether you did your job poorly, averagely or amazingly.

> ### Insight
> Expect cynicism. If all you write down is the bare minimum, a cynical reader can interpret this however they like:
>
> ▶ Stacking shelves at LIDL: Having a laugh seeing who could build the biggest pyramid of baked bean tins.
> ▶ Preparing mood boards for design presentations: Making patterns with coloured paper whenever feeling bored – or moody.
> ▶ Mixing cocktails: Mixing and drinking cocktails. Mixing some more. Drinking those as well.
> ▶ Answering the phone: Picking up the receiver, whimpering 'Leave me alone' and putting it down again.

Old job descriptions can be a very handy reminder, but don't just copy them out word for word. Find proof: for each responsibility you mention, think of an example of how you showed you were good at it.

Let's say you were a shelf stacker at a busy store. Or a 'shelf filler', or 'stock control assistant', or 'replenishment assistant': all are similar roles with similar duties.

All retailers want their shelf stackers to:

▶ prevent out of stocks so that customers don't go somewhere else to buy it
▶ keep shelves full and products attractively displayed to encourage sales
▶ help customers find anything they can't see, so they don't walk out without buying.

It's all about ensuring customers spend as much as possible when they are in the shop.

How can you show you understand this, and are (or were) good at this job?

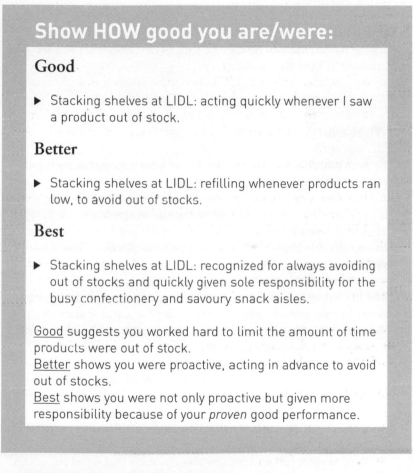

Show HOW good you are/were:

Good

▶ Stacking shelves at LIDL: acting quickly whenever I saw a product out of stock.

Better

▶ Stacking shelves at LIDL: refilling whenever products ran low, to avoid out of stocks.

Best

▶ Stacking shelves at LIDL: recognized for always avoiding out of stocks and quickly given sole responsibility for the busy confectionery and savoury snack aisles.

Good suggests you worked hard to limit the amount of time products were out of stock.
Better shows you were proactive, acting in advance to avoid out of stocks.
Best shows you were not only proactive but given more responsibility because of your *proven* good performance.

3 *DO YOU STILL DO WHAT YOU DID?*

What you *actually* do now (or did when you left the job) can be very different from the official job description for the position you originally accepted.

For example, you started out as an administrator, co-ordinating time sheets and invoices for contractors. Two years later, you took on extra responsibility for contractor payrolls and budgets. Six years on, with your boss on a year's maternity leave, you are now the acting financial manager and report directly to the director of the department.

If you stick to your old job description and title, you will be selling yourself short. Always be sure to describe what former jobs involved at their highest level.

What everyone wants

By now you should have a clear list of what you did in each job.

A great way to get into the right frame of mind for this next section is to think a bit more about what appeals to employers. Whatever kind of job you do or are looking for, there are certain 'generic' or transferable skills that most employers will value. The kinds of skills everyone wants.

The list below covers (in no particular order) ten valuable generic skills. In case you are not familiar with all of them, each one includes a brief explanation and some examples of how they might be used in a job or outside work.

As you read through each skill, try to think of some examples – however big or small – from your own life: from work, interests or family life.

Top ten generic skills

Make notes as you go through this exercise. This will help make sure you don't forget important examples when you write these out in full later.

These skills are in no particular order:

- Communication
- Interpersonal skills
- Time management
- Problem solving
- Creativity and innovation
- Motivation
- Initiative
- Analytical skills
- Flexibility
- Negotiation

If you are already familiar with all the above skills then by all means move straight on to 'Convince an employer of your skills' later in the chapter.

If you're not, the following pages give an explanation of each skill. Plenty of examples have been included to help you think about which skills you have and when you have used them.

COMMUNICATION

Communication is the ability to communicate information effectively to other people and receive it in return. It can be written, spoken or non-verbal.

Communication spans almost everything we do, and can include:

- writing your CV
- answering telephones and taking messages
- writing anything from emails to a technical handbook
- contributing to a meeting
- interviewing someone
- giving a sales presentation
- public speaking
- training staff
- persuading colleagues to help with a project
- serving customers at a bar

- demonstrating products
- listening to staff grievances
- explaining targets to a team
- understanding a client brief
- taking food orders in a restaurant
- explaining a bill to a customer or a solution to a problem
- working as a team to pass a ball and score a goal
- coaching a sports team
- helping a child understand what behaviour is expected of them
- writing school reports
- describing a dish for a menu.

The list is endless; while a few people do work pretty much in isolation, most of us communicate regularly in our work and our personal lives.

Even if you have never thought of yourself as a communicator, hopefully this list will prompt you to think of different ways that you have communicated – at work and at home – and to consider those times when you did it really well and made a difference.

INTERPERSONAL SKILLS (PEOPLE SKILLS)

In its most basic sense, this is the ability to get along with other people. At a higher level, it is being able to influence other people's mood and behaviour in a positive way.

It is quite closely related to how we communicate, and focuses almost as much on non-verbal as verbal communication. Building rapport or 'clicking' with new people quickly is a great example of strong people skills.

Other ways you can demonstrate people skills is by being able to:

- calm down someone who is angry or upset
- use humour (appropriately!) to defuse tension
- address difficult issues
- convince someone to act, or to buy something

- ▶ give feedback while avoiding confrontation
- ▶ inspire and motivate a team to achieve their goals
- ▶ offer support and sympathy to someone in need.

Anyone who spends time with other people at work or at home will need interpersonal skills to some extent. The more people you deal with successfully, the better your skills are likely to be.

As you look through your basic CV details, try to think of times you have used or developed your interpersonal skills to improve a situation or get a positive result.

TIME MANAGEMENT

Time management is being able to organize your time so you get through your tasks efficiently, while allowing time to handle any emergencies that might come up.

Good time management involves working out what you have to do each day and when to do it, so you don't leave the most important things until the last minute or rush around from crisis to crisis. Obviously some jobs are more challenging than others, but to do any job well requires some sense of time management, as do many non-work tasks.

Example: Do you time manage well?

A lorry driver plans her day to allow for refuelling, tachograph stops and a lunch break, working out the best place and time to do each so that the worst traffic is avoided, delivery slots are hit, and legal requirements are met. Good time management.

Catering a three-course lunch for 20 people requires careful planning, preparation and co-ordinating of cooking processes to ensure everyone gets hot food at the same time.

(Contd)

A personal assistant needs to issue a daily diary, organize a conference, type letters, fill out an expense report, print slides for a meeting and arrange for samples to be sent by same-day courier; do you manage a day filled with similar activities?

Students writing four essays in one month, with each essay needing different research and practical work, all due in on the same day, along with rugby practice and event committee meetings (and of course bar time, but don't mention that here), need time management skills to get everything done.

Getting four children up, dressed, breakfasted and off to different nurseries and schools on time in the morning is another excellent example of time management skill.

Again, going through your list of basic employment details should help you remember some good examples of where you have shown time management skills. Make a note of these.

PROBLEM SOLVING

This is exactly what it says on the tin – solving problems. Almost everyone does this, at home or at work.

Not surprisingly, employers really appreciate people who come up with ways to help them carry out their business more efficiently and profitably, or in a more appealing or environmentally friendly way, all the while managing to keep customers happy.

Examples of solving problems include:

- ▶ Stopping soup tins jamming on a conveyor belt.
- ▶ Finding an alternative route that beats the traffic.
- ▶ Changing a filing system to save time looking for lost records.
- ▶ Coming up with a way to make an unprofitable product profitable.
- ▶ Devising a food and drink promotion to get enough customers in at lunchtimes.

- Setting up an FAQ web page to handle excessive customer enquiries.
- Figuring out why a computer stopped working and fixing it.
- Helping a child handle a difficult situation with a friend.
- Introducing subscription fees to a sports club to safeguard practice facilities.
- Developing a faster way to pick and pack stock in a warehouse.
- Finding an emergency replacement for someone who is sick.
- Devising an incentive scheme to bring sales up to target levels.
- Changing a venue from outdoors to indoors due to bad weather.

You should be able to come up with many examples from your own work (or your interests or home life) when you take a bit of time to think through each job and what you did for each employer.

Those you eventually include in your CV will, of course, be the most powerful and relevant examples. For the purpose of this stage, note down as many examples as you can.

CREATIVITY AND INNOVATION

These terms are often misconstrued. For CV purposes, being creative doesn't just have to mean you are brilliantly artistic. Creative or innovative thinking means approaching things from a new angle, seeing and doing things differently, finding links between different things or, in its most basic form, creating something new.

Creativity is often sparked by a desire to solve a problem or make improvements. It is therefore frequently mentioned as a useful approach to problem solving, although not all problem solving has to be creative: it can just as easily be logical and methodical.

You might have used your creativity when you:

- thought up a way to restock shelves faster or more efficiently
- worked out how to waste less cardboard when packaging products

- came up with a new product or service that no other company currently offers
- had a great idea for attracting more customers to the wine bar in the afternoon
- found a way to share advertising costs with retailers and increase sales together.

When creativity is actually put into practice, like developing a new product or introducing a new business process, it's often referred to as innovation. Almost any successful new way of doing something could be considered innovative.

MOTIVATION

All employers want to employ motivated staff: people whom they believe will work hard in the best interests of the company.

Motivation can be shown in many ways. It might be someone who:

- comes in a little early or leaves a little late to get a task finished
- gets their job done as fast and well as possible
- is keen to get involved in new projects
- thinks about a problem over the weekend, suggesting a solution on Monday
- takes on work beyond their job description to help the business succeed
- talks to customers with enthusiasm about company products or services
- gets people around them excited about the work that they do
- looks forward to their working day and to making a difference.

Even if you don't feel inspired by the work that you do, you can still be motivated to do a good job. Think of examples to show how your motivation has benefited employers.

INITIATIVE

An employee who spots something that needs to be done, and then does it without being asked, is showing initiative.

Most employers love this positive trait as they know that employees with initiative are not often sitting around unproductive. Whenever they are free, they will be looking for ways to benefit the business.

Examples

When the production line breaks down and an engineer takes half an hour to fix it, the person with initiative spends time folding extra boxes to avoid delays in packing later on; they don't just wait or take an extra rest break.

Other good examples of initiative are:

▶ The PA who provisionally books a conference venue while his manager is off sick.
▶ The engineer who invites herself onto a project team because she has some ideas.
▶ The person who acts to prevent an accident or crisis.

Someone who uses initiative will always be more attractive to employers as they can work independently and add value by themselves, rather than needing a colleague or manager to watch over and direct all their actions throughout the day.

ANALYTICAL SKILLS

This is looking at information in a logical way and, based on it, making a sensible decision. Analytical skills may sound advanced, but they are something we all use in our day-to-day lives. They are what you use in the following situations:

Buying a car

You might read reports on ten different cars that you like the look of, take four for a test drive and then, based on the cost and what you feel you are getting for your money (trim, servicing, optional extras, finance) decide which is the best one to buy.

Planning a wedding venue

Your final decision might be influenced by several pieces of information:

▶ how much money you want to spend
▶ how many guests you want to invite
▶ where guests will be travelling from
▶ proximity to airports, train stations, bus stations, etc.
▶ whether guests need to stay overnight
▶ the groom's or bride's opinion
▶ your mother's opinion
▶ your mother-in-law's opinion.

Examples

For these examples at work, the decision you make is based on analytical skills:

1 You are trying to work out whether sales are down because a product is not good, or because people have stopped buying it due to economic pressures. You might need to look into:

▶ your main competitor's sales record with a similar product
▶ overall industry performance
▶ recent customer feedback
▶ what your sales team is saying.

With this information, you may decide to stop selling the product, upgrade it, or offer it at a discount.

2 You are the manager of a busy bar and see that on Fridays and Saturdays, when you run out of alcopops well before closing time, customers buy lower cost beers instead, so you are missing out on potential profit. You decide to stock more alcopops on Fridays and Saturdays and profits rise. However, there are more fights as well. The cost of repairing the bar is higher than your increase in profits, and you don't want to get a bad reputation in town.

So you return to your original alcopop stock levels and expect to sell out on weekends.

FLEXIBILITY

This is another trait that really appeals to employers – the ability (and willingness) to respond to changing situations. This might involve working in a different way, or learning new skills. 'Adaptability' is a term sometimes used instead of flexibility.

Covering for someone else while they are off sick, on holiday or on maternity leave, is often a way to show flexibility – perhaps you took on a different type of work, or increased your overall workload and delegated some of your work to someone else.

Attending training courses or gaining further qualifications while working also suggests flexibility; you are not focusing purely on the same narrow field of work all the time. If you temp successfully in a variety of roles for different companies and managers, you are also showing great flexibility.

Other examples of flexibility include:

▶ relocating
▶ retraining
▶ taking on additional responsibilities
▶ learning a language
▶ developing a new skill
▶ moving sideways in the company.

Working flexible hours is not usually a good example of being flexible; in this example, the flexibility tends to come from the employer, not the employee!

NEGOTIATION

Negotiation is not about getting what you want. It's about working towards agreement: individuals, teams or companies with different aims finding a common solution that works for all parties.

Skilled negotiators are able to shape their own work and that of people around them (be they customers or colleagues), while ensuring everyone feels satisfied with the outcome.

You don't have to be a hostage negotiator or a buyer in a large company for negotiation to be a useful skill. Employers welcome this skill at every level.

Example

On a basic level, negotiation can be this simple:

Your boss approaches you with an important and urgent task. You already have your hands full with another task. So you say, 'If you give me two more days to submit my weekly report, then I can get this done by the end of tomorrow.'

Your boss is pleased: the task will be done.

You're happy too, as you won't have to work until midnight to get the weekly report done as well.

That's successful negotiation.

In general, negotiating skills are increasingly useful to an employer the higher you rise within their organization. Your job title might not say negotiator, but if you are a manager representing a team or department working on a project, or in an interdepartmental meeting, negotiation skills are often an advantage.

Employers recruiting into sales or other customer-facing functions will often find negotiation skills particularly appealing.

Even if your job has never involved negotiation and you can't think of any times you have used this skill, remember that job offers, appraisals and promotions also tend to involve negotiations.

If you are employed, the chances are you have done some sort of negotiation to gain your current role. This negotiation may have covered things like:

▶ salary and benefits
▶ flexible working hours
▶ incentives/bonuses
▶ working from home
▶ agreeing performance targets
▶ the responsibilities you will take on
▶ opportunities for promotion
▶ what training you would like to receive.

Convince an employer of your skills

Now you understand what the most wanted skills are, it's time to write down the ones you know you possess. But it's not enough to simply tell an employer you have certain skills. The key to being convincing on your CV is not just to say which skills you have, but to show how you have used them.

Go back through each job in your factsheet, starting with your most recent job, and try to think of examples of how and when you have shown each of the ten skills.

Actions speak louder than words

When you think of examples, write down specific actions you have performed and results you have achieved. Focus on using verbs – action words – to describe them.

Explain what you did, made, suggested, improved, showed, tried or changed. Don't worry too much about which action word makes you sound best just yet. This is still your private factsheet, so just include as much detail as you can remember. You'll be refining it later on.

If you have been working for many years, focus on your most recent two or three roles when thinking of examples. If you have hopped around from job to job or company to company, focus on the most recent three to five years.

Don't ignore examples from outside work: these can prove useful in anyone's CV, but are particularly relevant for school leavers and graduates with little or no work experience, or for those returning from a career break.

Once you have thought of an example, put it into the right section of your factsheet: Employment or Work Experience, Education or Interests. If it is work related, make sure it is against the right company and the right job.

Your summary of examples could look like this for a holiday job, or your first job after leaving school. Action words are in **bold**.

Example

Aug 2009–Nov 2009   Ride Host, Scary Mary's
                           Entertainment Park

Communication: Explaining ride safety rules to park guests. **Working** with operators to shut down rides

quickly/safely if guests break rules or when something goes wrong.

Interpersonal skills: Using humour and friendly authority to **encourage** everyone, especially teenagers, to respect the rules. **Managing** queue line fights when rides break down/long delays. **Calming** angry parents whose children are too short to ride safely despite having queued; **persuading** them to leave the ride quickly to avoid delays.

Time management: Turning up on time for every handover: **avoiding** delays to rides from not having enough hosts.

Problem solving: Sorting out problems with guests and equipment, **keeping** ride queues moving as fast as possible. **Handling** ill people, scared children, over- and under-sized people, breakdowns, lost property, fights, fast track riders, single riders, and people changing their minds at the last minute.

Creativity and innovation: Little room for creativity here – they want everyone to follow health and safety rulebook ... **Changing** ride announcements to make them more entertaining.

Motivation: Arriving early to help with test rides before the park opens. **Enjoy** the work: love watching people's faces when they get off a ride for the first time.

(Contd)

Initiative: When the Vomit Comet and the tannoy broke down in August with a huge queue, **decided** to go down the queue line in person **telling** everyone why there was a delay and how long it was likely to be, to **keep people calm** and so they could leave for another ride if they wanted. **Helped** keep levels of complaints and staff abuse down.

Analytical skills: Working with hosts, operators and engineers to **agree** when a ride is safe to reopen.

Flexibility: Was employed to work on Death's Breath, but always **volunteered** to cover other rides when busy or short staffed. In three months have **hosted** every ride in the park; am now the first person asked for whenever there's a problem with the staff roster.

Negotiation: When offered the job, **getting** my employee annual pass upgraded to include Dead Fred's HorrorLand and Whizz Kidz Adventureworld by **agreeing** to work late shifts.

Specialist skills

Along with the generic skills listed above, there may be some specific or specialist skills and experience that you will need in order to do a job effectively. Some might be essential, others just an added bonus.

Here is a list of random examples of specialist skills:

- ▶ Administration
- ▶ Bookkeeping
- ▶ Computer
- ▶ Diagnostic
- ▶ Editing

- French
- Graphic design
- Horse riding
- Interviewing
- Journalism
- Knife throwing
- Leadership
- Medical
- Numeracy
- Origination
- Public relations
- Quality management
- Research
- Selling
- Typesetting
- Unix
- Veterinary
- Web
- X-raying
- Yodelling
- Zookeeping

For any specialist skills you possess, go through the same 'proof' process as for your generic skills. Note down every example you can think of.

Your CV factsheet should now contain examples of how you have shown all the skills an employer could possibly wish to see. Some examples will shine brighter than others, but don't try to filter any out just yet.

TEN THINGS TO REMEMBER

1 *Past performance is how employers will predict future performance.*

2 *Your Employment section is critical, if you have one.*

3 *Job responsibilities don't show an employer how well you did a job.*

4 *Assume all CV readers are cynical: brief does not mean bare minimum.*

5 *Focus on the ten generic skills that every employer wants.*

6 *Prove the contribution you've made by giving real examples.*

7 *Examples should include your actions and the benefit to your employer.*

8 *Generic skills can take examples from work and home life.*

9 *Include proof of specialist skills using examples from work.*

10 *Don't edit anything yet: just write down as many examples as you can think of.*

4

....

How to SHORTlist your best points

In this chapter you will:

- *learn to SHORTlist examples: prove skills in a distinctive, personal way*
- *use SHORTlisting to write your Profile, Employment History and more*

_____

What makes a good example?

When you go back and read them, some of your examples describing how you have shown key skills might seem a bit weak. It could be that you aren't very practised at this skill – but more often, it's because the example you've given is not specific enough.

For every example that you've noted, you need to check whether it is specific enough to add power to your CV. This next process, called SHORTlisting, will help you transform woolly examples into concise proof of your skills.

SHORTlisted examples make it clear why you should be asked for interview. They are your starting point for everything that follows in your job search: they form the basis of your CVs, application forms and covering letters, and help you right up to interview stage.

How do I SHORTlist my examples?

Every example needs to be as SHORT as it can be:

- ▶ Specific: what exactly did you do, why and how?
- ▶ Honest: did <u>you</u> do it? Alone or as part of a team (what part did you play)?
- ▶ Outcome: was there a measurable result or benefit for your employer?
- ▶ Realistic: does what you are claiming sound achievable – or like a fantasy?
- ▶ Transferable: will this skill be useful to any future employer?

Let's take each aspect in turn.

Specific

Use details or numbers to explain exactly what you are talking about.

Example

A sales administrator responsible for compiling reports for the sales director every month wants to show he has good communication skills as his next step is moving into sales.

Good

- ▶ Reporting on sales expenses.

He states clearly what he is reporting on.
But what kind of report is it, how often does he do it, does it need input from other people?

Better

▶ Comparing year-on-year sales expenses, reporting to the sales director every month end.

He is now stating exactly what his reporting involves. It's still not clear how big a task this is and whether he does it alone.

Best

▶ Solely responsible for working with the 30-strong sales team to understand year-on-year sales expense trends, reporting to the sales director every month end.

This covers all the bases about size and scope, what he does and with whom he does it.

Honest

Do what it says on the tin: be honest.

Use an example only if it shows something you have actually done. Don't position yourself as having done something if you did not; nor should you take full credit for something you did as part of a team.

It can be tempting to claim a few extra things to make yourself sound better; but if you do get invited to interview on that basis, your story could collapse under questioning or be undermined when your former employer sends in their reference.

There's no Good, Better, Best example for this point: only you know whether or not you are being honest.

Outcome

This is one of the most essential pieces of information you can include: what difference your actions made to the company. This should ideally be measurable and could be:

- ▶ a sales or profit increase
- ▶ more customers coming through the door
- ▶ a reduction in wastage
- ▶ saving of time or money
- ▶ improvement in morale or relationships
- ▶ achievement of an award
- ▶ greater customer satisfaction
- ▶ more hits on a website, etc.

Think back to the sales administrator using his communication skills to reduce and report upon sales expenses. Fortunately for him, some things are easier to measure than others – and costs are one such thing.

Example

Good

Sole responsibility for working with the 30-strong sales team to understand and control year-on-year sales expenses, reporting to the sales director every month end.

Better

Sole responsibility for working with the 30-strong sales team to understand and control their year-on-year sales expenses, reporting monthly savings to the sales director.

Best

Sole responsibility for assisting the 30-strong sales team to understand and control their sales expenses, reporting an average monthly saving of 5% to the sales director.

ESTIMATING YOUR IMPACT

There may be some occasions when you simply can't put a figure to the difference that you've made: but you can often sensibly estimate one if you think about it.

Example: you have done something that speeds up a process

Work out how much time it will save one person each time the process is performed. Multiply that by the number of times it is done, and the number of people doing it, per day/week/month. That will be your total time saving per day/week/month.

Let's say you worked out a way to stop bottles on a conveyor system from jamming when the turntable got full. The bottles used to jam every 30 minutes or so when a new batch came through; the line had to stop for five minutes each time to sort it out.

Now, after making your change, it never jams. What measurable difference did you make?

In an 8-hour day, the line would jam twice an hour: about 16 times.

(Contd)

16 stoppages for 5 minutes each time: 16 x 5 = 80 minutes per day.

In a working month (22 days) you save 80 mins x 22 days = 1760 minutes per month. That's almost 30 hours.

So, you can say you've saved your employer 30 hours' production time every month.

Realistic

Put yourself in the shoes of the person reading your CV. Does the example you've used to demonstrate your skill sound realistic?

If it does, great. If it doesn't, check whether you have made a typing error or have overestimated, exaggerated or outright lied.

DOES THE SCOPE OF YOUR RESPONSIBILITY SOUND REALISTIC?

For example, if your job title states 'Marketing Assistant' and one of your examples reads:

Single-handedly managing the successful launch campaign for Chocopigs, the biggest new brand of the decade.

readers of your CV might take the cynical view that you have exaggerated. Few corporations would give sole responsibility for a major new product launch to an assistant, so you may need to tone down your language slightly:

Single-handedly managing all the consumer and market research that formed the basis of the successful launch campaign for major new brand Chocopigs.

Or, if it happens to be true and you were in fact given a lot of responsibility within your company, or it was a one-off opportunity, then make this clear, for example:

Winning promotion to single-handedly co-ordinate the launch campaign for a major new brand, Chocopigs, while the marketing manager was on sick leave.

DOES THE OUTCOME YOU CLAIM TO HAVE ACHIEVED SOUND REALISTIC?

For example, you worked as an administrator for a small family business. Your example of creativity says you improved the way accounts were filed so they could be found faster, saving your employer eight man hours per month. Instinctively this sounds quite realistic.

If you claim to have radically overhauled the accounts filing system to save your employer eight man hours per week, it is more of a stretch but could still be possible – if the changes were significant or the accounts are searched regularly.

If you claim to have saved your employer 80 man hours per week through changes to the filing system, alarm bells will probably start ringing – 80 hours is two people's fulltime jobs.

If you are not confident in your number skills or aren't comfortable with the number you've calculated, ask for help from a friend or colleague who is good with numbers.

If our sales administrator had a typo in his CV which said he'd been solely responsible for achieving a 50 per cent reduction in sales expenses every month, chances are the reader would either discard the CV for exaggeration, or would discover his error during the interview.

Coming unstuck at interview won't just invalidate one example, it will throw all your claims and examples into doubt. Always check your examples are realistic.

Transferable

Where your examples show generic skills, they should not need any further work. Generic skills are, by definition, transferable to any role and therefore useful to any employer.

However, you may also have examples of more specialist skills, which – unless you think laterally – may only be truly transferable if you are looking for work within the same field. Obviously for specialist skills, your example can only be SHOR at most. The same example could if necessary be tweaked to show off a different skill, one that is more relevant.

Example

Our talented sales administrator decides he is looking for a change of direction. He's no longer interested in being a salesperson; the job he wants next is regional training manager for a national retailer, working with staff in 25 different stores to help them increase profitability.

When comparing expense reports to help the sales team reduce their sales expenses, he was using analytical and financial skills. By saving the company money, he also contributed to their profits. By playing up the financial aspects of the same example, he can use it to show off different skills and experience.

Good

Analysing sales expense reports to help reduce costs by 5% year on year.

Better

Analysing sales expense reports and helping the sales team reduce their sales expenses, successfully achieving a 5% reduction in expenses year on year.

Best

Analysing sales expense reports and providing basic financial training to the 30-strong account team to help them reduce account expenses, increasing annual profits by 2%.

The best example now shows off his analytical skills, financial understanding, training ability and his contribution to company profitability.

Starting with your own examples

The quick way to check how strong your examples are is to note an S, H, O, R and T against each one if it definitely meets that requirement.

Example

You have been personal assistant to the vice presidents of a national company for two years. The job has been good and the two VPs are great bosses, but there's no opportunity for promotion. A similar role with a bigger, international company would be ideal.

(Contd)

Time management is an essential skill for doing your job well, and something you know you are good at. Your first example to prove this skill is:

Good

▶ Managing a diary effectively to make optimum use of time.

Specific? **No.** You aren't showing who you do this for, or how well.
Honest? **Yes.** Your time management is definitely effective.
Outcome? **No.** What benefit does your great time management give to the company?
Realistic? **You** haven't made any specific claims yet.
Transferable? **Yes.** Time management is a useful generic skill.

So this example is only **H T** at best. It's still a bit too much like a job description: 'The successful applicant must manage senior managers' diaries effectively.' It doesn't say exactly what you've done or the impact it had: you are completely missing **S** and **O**, which also makes **R** impossible to check.

Better

▶ Saving two Vice Presidents time every month by balancing effective diary management with ad-hoc tasks such as conference organization for up to 200 delegates.

Specific? **Yes**. You've now mentioned supporting two VPs with other specific tasks.
Realistic? **So far**. Check again once **O**utcome is stronger.
Outcome? **No.** It's better, as you've mentioned saving time, but still not specific enough.

This is now **S H R T**: **O** is still rather weak.

Best

▶ Saving two VPs one day a month with more effective diary management, while personally arranging four international conferences for up to 200 delegates – one awarded 'Best of 2008'.

Specific? **Yes**. Four international conferences and co-ordinating diaries for two VPs.
Honest? **Yes**, if you truly did all the above yourself.
Outcome? **Yes**. You've saved a measurable amount of time each month (which has a value to the company) and been recognized for your conference organization skill.
Realistic? **Yes**. Although not if you'd claimed to have done all this in just six months.
Transferable? **Yes**. This shows you can successfully balance lots of different tasks.

This is now **SHORT** and can be listed as a finished bullet point on your factsheet.

You may, after going through all parts of this process, find you just can't make an example properly **SHORT**. Despite your best efforts, it is still missing one or more areas. Don't discard it: just mark clearly the areas it does meet, such as **SHRT**, and move on. At the end, you may find it's still the best example you can come up with for that skill. Once you've SHORTlisted all your examples, the best ones to use for each CV you write will be obvious.

TEN THINGS TO REMEMBER

1 *Start by putting yourself in the employer's shoes.*

2 *Anyone can claim anything: claims do not make a powerful CV.*

3 *Employers need proof based on real-life examples.*

4 *Refine your examples by SHORTlisting.*

5 *Specific examples are more convincing.*

6 *Total honesty is essential.*

7 *Outcomes help employers understand how your skills could benefit them.*

8 *Outlandish claims undermine a CV: keep examples realistic.*

9 *Focus on transferable, generic skills in most of your examples.*

10 *Don't delete examples that aren't fully SHORT: they may still come in useful.*

5

Prioritizing the essentials

In this chapter you will:
- *understand what employers really want to know*
- *make it easy for employers to find that information first*

It's time to understand just what an employer is going to do with your CV. To do that, you need to know who is reading your CV – or at least, what is important to them.

Whoever reads your CV will be working under two main constraints: time and knowledge.

Time constraints

Most people are under time constraints at work; no one is ever going to take as much time to read your CV as you hope they will. This can seem unfair given the effort you are going to, but if you make it easy for someone to quickly see why you should be shortlisted for interview (or why your CV shouldn't go in the bin), then all the effort will have been worth it.

Insight

If 100 people applied for a vacancy and each CV took five minutes to read, it would take the reader an entire day (without breaks) to read them all. That's on top of their normal job.

(Contd)

It would take a week to get through 500 applications. What if there were four vacancies at once, not one? No one can take a month out of their job to do nothing but read CVs.

That's why you'll be lucky if anyone spends more than two minutes reading your CV. Even a whole minute should be considered a gift: many readers decide in seconds.

Time constraints are partly why many employers turn to recruitment agencies to help them fill vacancies. Hurray, you might think: an agency will read my CV properly! After all, that's what they do for a living. But in fact it isn't much easier for recruitment agents.

Reading CVs is most definitely a part of a recruitment agent's job, but they also have research, interviews, client meetings, negotiations and internal issues to handle – and often they will be dealing with many different clients and vacancies.

So don't be fooled into thinking that sending a CV to a recruitment agency instead of an employer – whether speculatively or for an advertised vacancy – means you can submit something longer, or less finished. True, many recruitment agencies rewrite selected CVs in their preferred style (or that of their clients), but they may not bother rewriting yours and passing it on if they can't easily see what you have to offer their clients.

Some companies save time by using automated CV scanning to sift through the first round of applications by computer, only giving real people CVs to read once this initial shortlist is over. This is also something you will need to take into account; more detail on this can be found in Part four, Targeting it carefully.

To suit time constraints, your CV needs to be **brief** and **relevant**.

Knowledge constraints

The other thing to keep in mind is that the first people to read your CV may not be those you will be interviewed by or end up working for.

Within many small to medium-sized companies, it could well be the manager who has the vacancy who reads the CVs. In larger companies with a Human Resources (HR) manager or department, it is most likely someone from the HR team who will process the CVs, at least to start with. Or the reader may be a recruitment agent. Even if a job advert tells you to send your CV to a named manager, it may still be filtered through HR first.

So, it's safest to assume that your first reader is someone who does not do the job you are applying to do and may not work in the same field. This means they may have little, if any, specialist knowledge of the role or any similar ones you have done in the past.

To account for these knowledge constraints, your CV needs to use plain English – ideally no jargon unless it is specifically mentioned in the job advertisement.

Start as you mean to go on

Your skill examples, properly SHORTlisted, will be brief, relevant and in plain English.

That's good.

They are also buried in your Employment History.

Not so good.

How can you make sure someone so short of time reads enough of your CV to make sure they see all these brilliant examples?

You can't. But you can make it easy for them by giving your highlights at the start.

Most CVs these days start with a short summary of who you are and what you offer an employer: a miniature introduction, if you like. Rather than just laying claim to a long list of skills, this is where you point out your best skills and direct the reader to the rest of your CV for proof (your SHORTlisted examples).

The focus of this summary can be:

▶ **Your skills.** It could be called your Profile, Summary, Skills Profile, Skills Summary, Key Skills, Professional Profile or Professional Summary.
▶ **Your achievements.** This might be headed Achievements – although you can call it Personal Achievements or Professional Achievements if you want to distinguish between them.
▶ **A mixture of your Skills and Achievements.** This could simply be called your Profile, Summary, Professional Profile or Professional Summary.

Exactly what you call it is up to you. If in doubt, something simple such as Summary, Profile or Key Skills is probably the safest option. Using the word 'Professional' is probably inappropriate if you have little or no work experience or you don't work in a professional field.

Converting SHORTlisted examples into a summary

Two simple steps will create your Summary:

1 Decide which five skills are your priorities.
2 Select your best example bullet points.

PRIORITIES

The five skills you choose should closely match the job description or the general field you are applying for. If you don't have a job advert in mind, are preparing your CV well in advance, or want to think about a new direction, you will probably need to revisit this later when creating your CV for a specific job application.

Example

You want an international sales job, selling advanced electronic communications equipment to airport contractors. Your top five skill priorities are:

▶ Interpersonal skills (generic)
▶ Communication skills (generic)
▶ Negotiation skills (generic)
▶ Creativity (generic)
▶ Industry/product knowledge (specialist).

SELECT YOUR BULLET POINTS

Go through your employment history and pull out all the bullet points that demonstrate the five skills you have prioritized. Pick the single strongest, **SHORT**est example for each of the five skills.

Example

Interpersonal skills (generic)

Contractor Manager, Hub Airport

▶ Smoothing day-to-day relationships between contractors during the opening upheaval at Terminal 6, minimizing customer impact and enabling 90% of flights to depart on time.

(Contd)

Communication skills (generic)

Office Administrator, Fly By Wire

▶ Writing humorous yet appropriate editorial and collating articles for the biannual company newsletter, gaining a strong enough readership in six countries to justify a quarterly issue.

Negotiation skills (generic)

Store Manager, Gadgets Galore

▶ Leading negotiations between contractors and head office to alter the site refurbishment schedule; completing a radical overhaul just one month late and without any fall in sales.

Creativity (generic)

Deputy Store Manager, Gadgets Galore

▶ Increasing seasonal footfall by renting three eye-catching soundproofed pods for testing the latest electronic gadgetry; increasing post-Christmas profits by 18 per cent year on year.

Industry/product knowledge (specialist)

▶ Extensive personal network of more than 126 airport contractor contacts, based in London, Paris and New York.
▶ Four years' experience in electronics sales.

Possible three-sentence Summary:

Four years' experience successfully managing airport contractor relationships and building an extensive network of industry contacts places me in a position of strength. Proven sales and negotiation skills have helped me to maintain and even increase retail electronics sales during difficult seasonal periods. My creative approach to winning new business, exemplified by the gadget pod, delivers not just sales turnover but also profitability.

Now you have two options. You can edit them into:

▶ a brief bulleted list
▶ a short prose summary.

Which option you choose is down to you. Some people stick to bullets all the way; others like to vary their CV style by alternating prose and bullet points. Provided the end result still contains specific evidence to support your claims, it really doesn't matter.

Bulleted summary

If you decide on a bulleted list:

▶ keep it brief: it's called 'highlights' for a reason
▶ don't waste CV space by repeating yourself word for word.

ADVANTAGES

Bulleted lists are quick and easy to scan through.

A CV that starts with a bulleted list of skills or achievements will have a hybrid feel to it: this could help win over any recruiters who prefer a functional style (skills-based) CV.

DISADVANTAGES

Almost all your CV will be bullet points, making it harder for different sections to stand out.

It's harder to show any sense of personality in bullet points.

Example

- **Interpersonal skills:** Smoothly managing contractors at Hub Airport during the troublesome opening of Terminal 6, to keep 90 per cent of flights departing on time.
- **Communication:** The most popular editor of the biannual company newsletter, gaining sufficient readership in six countries to justify a quarterly issue.
- **Negotiation:** As store manager, negotiating with contractors and head office to delay a refurbishment schedule, avoiding the otherwise inevitable drop in sales.
- **Creativity:** Increased post-Christmas profits by 18 per cent while testing a new idea to drive seasonal retail footfall into gadget store; renting three eye-catching consumer 'test pods'.
- **Added value:** An extensive network of more than 100 airport contractor contacts based in London, Paris and New York, plus four years' experience in electronics sales.

Prose summary

If you decide on a prose summary:

- Combine and edit your examples into three or four sentences at most
- Ensure you retain concrete proof for at least your two best skills
- Include in your Employment section any specifics you had to edit out.

ADVANTAGES

It varies the layout of your CV, making it easy to distinguish between different sections.

Prose makes it easier to inject a little of your personality into the summary.

DISADVANTAGES

Starting a CV with a prose profile or summary may be more of a risk, as so many are done poorly and sound identical. The writer is a 'committed, dedicated, motivated, enthusiastic employee who is just brilliant at everything'. High on claims and low on proof, such profiles are empty and meaningless – and all too common. Some recruiters have become cynical about prose profiles and so may give them less weight, but keeping proof of your skills at the core of your summary should overcome their prejudice.

Example

Four years' experience successfully managing airport contractor relationships at Hub Airport and building an extensive network of industry contacts places me in a position of strength. My creative approach to attracting new customers, exemplified by the success of test pods at Gadgets Galore, delivers not just sales turnover but also profitability. Proven sales and negotiation skills have helped me to maintain and increase retail electronics sales during traditionally low-performing periods.

'I' or 'he/she'?

There appears to be a prevailing belief that, particularly on professional CVs, a prose summary should be written in the third person, i.e. referring to 'he' or 'she'.

The reason most often given for this is to avoid having every sentence starting with 'I' as this can sound a bit self-important, although you can avoid this by phrasing things in a different way. Some people also find it feels less like they are blowing their own trumpet when they write about themselves as if they were someone else.

Example: Third person

A charismatic, visionary manager capable of attracting high calibre staff from within and without the organization. Her proven skills include managing turbulent change as well as peak performance, as evidenced by the recent successful merger with competitor GlobalGreen, during which share prices rose unabated and staff morale was at an all-time high. She possesses a powerful combination of technical brilliance, long-term strategic insight and an easy-going management style – reflected in the 99% staff retention rates and rising profits at all five companies under her stewardship during the past 20 years.

Example: First person

I am a charismatic, visionary manager capable of attracting high calibre staff from within and without an organization. As evidenced by the recent successful merger with competitor GlobalGreen, during which share prices rose unabated and staff morale was at an all-time high, my proven skills include managing turbulent change as well as peak performance. I possess a powerful combination of technical brilliance, long-term strategic insight and an easy-going management style – reflected in the 99% staff retention rates and rising profits at all five of the companies under my stewardship during the past 20 years.

Using the third person he/she approach could seem over-formal and stuffy, especially when writing a non-professional CV. Writing about yourself as 'him' or 'her' may feel impersonal, strange or pompous to you. Although each recruiter no doubt has a personal preference, you are unlikely to put them off by writing in the style you feel most comfortable with.

It could be argued that the above example reads marginally more convincingly and less arrogantly in the third person, probably due to the seniority of the professional concerned. However, a student might approach things differently.

Example

Good

This talented Psychology student at Bristol University is due to graduate in July 2010 with a predicted 2:1. He possesses excellent time management skills which, along with his reliability and honesty, have helped him to hold down the same bar job throughout his entire degree course. He also plays football at University level – last season as treasurer and this season as captain of an as yet unbeaten side – showing he can work well as part of a team.

It sounds a bit over the top in the third person. First person can be more personable:

Better

I am a talented Psychology student at Bristol University and I am due to graduate in July 2010 with a predicted 2:1. I possess excellent time management skills which, along with my reliability and honesty, have helped me to hold down the same bar job throughout my entire degree course. I also play football at University level – last season
(Contd)

as treasurer and this season as captain of an as yet
unbeaten side – showing I can work well as part of a team.

This comes across a bit stilted, with lots of 'I's. A simple
rewrite is all that's needed:

Best

A talented Psychology student at Bristol University, I am due
to graduate in July 2010 with a predicted 2:1. Excellent time
management skills, along with reliability and honesty, have
helped me to hold down the same bar job throughout my entire
degree course. Playing football at University level – last season
as treasurer and this season as captain of an as yet unbeaten
side – proves my ability to work well as part of a team.

Be consistent

Whichever style you pick, make sure you use the same one throughout
your summary – don't change halfway through. As 'I' tends to come
more naturally when we talk or write about ourselves, it probably
makes sense to use 'I' as your default. A concise, note-style way of
writing (as in the example above) and varied sentence structures mean
you can use the first person without saying 'I' too much.

Example

Rather than:

I have developed great communication and interpersonal
skills through my voluntary work as a fundraiser for a local
hospice. I can get people excited about my ideas and keen
to try them out. I devised a sheep-painting fundraiser

last month which was supported by staff, local farmers and tradespeople. I broke the hospice record for the most money raised at one event.

Try:

Great communication and interpersonal skills, gained through fundraising for a local hospice, help get people excited about my creative ideas and keen to try them out. My sheep-painting fundraiser last month was supported by staff, local farmers and tradespeople, and broke the hospice record for most money raised at one event.

Avoid ending up with a mishmash of styles, like this:

A member of the Institute of Civil Engineers, I possess over ten years' tunnelling experience specializing in the application of shotcrete. Refined leadership and communication skills enable him to successfully manage diverse teams of more than 50 people. My perfect safety record over 14 consecutive projects is a significant achievement while never falling behind schedule.

Once you've completed your edited bullets or three sentences of prose, that's the first draft of your Profile or Summary done. Don't worry if it doesn't sound quite finished yet: as usual, you will be refining it later anyway so will have a chance to revisit it.

Add your highlights at the top of your factsheet, underneath your personal details. Your factsheet should now be starting to look like a basic CV.

TEN THINGS TO REMEMBER

1 *The person reading your CV will be short of time.*

2 *Be brief and relevant so you can be assessed quickly.*

3 *The person reading your CV may not do the same job as you.*

4 *Write in plain English to suit any reader.*

5 *Spotlight your strengths with a Summary/Profile at the top of your CV.*

6 *Summary/Profile can be bullet points or a short paragraph.*

7 *Do not include lists of 'businessy' adjectives and empty claims.*

8 *Talk about yourself, in your own language.*

9 *Always keep the focus on* **proof**.

10 *Be consistent in your writing style.*

Part three

Refining your language

Part three shows you how to transform your factsheet into a proper CV.

Refining is about choosing the best possible words and phrases: ones that 'lift' your CV from the pile. Words can genuinely make you stand out from other people who have a similar – or even better – education, work history and skill set from your own.

The refining stage also suggests ways to smooth out trouble spots so they are less noticeable, while keeping your CV honest so you don't land yourself in trouble later. There's also advice on how much industry jargon you can safely include and where to draw the line.

If you've already written a CV and checked the contents of each section against the previous chapters, this is when you will start to make it truly effective.

6

Effective language to make you stand out

In this chapter you will:

- **understand why your choice of words is so important**
- **choose the most powerful action words to suit you**
- **refine the language in your CV**

How you approach this aspect of CV writing depends largely on how you feel about language.

Some people deliberately ignore this stage: they feel confident that their concrete achievements and proven abilities speak for themselves, and don't appreciate how essential good writing is.

Others simply don't understand what this part involves and therefore can't see why it is so important.

There are also those who recognize good writing when they see it, but for some reason aren't able to replicate it themselves.

The basic rules of CV writing

There are three basic points that it helps to understand before you start:

1 The most critical words on your CV are those you start each section or bullet point with. These will be the first – and possibly the only – words read by an employer or recruiter who quickly scans through your CV. They should be verbs – action words.

2 Most, if not all, CV writers and readers would agree that the words you use to describe yourself speak volumes about you as a person. This is especially true of the verbs – or action words – that you include in your CV.

3 Impressive words or 'management speak' are not the foundation of a well-written CV. Just think carefully about the words you choose and, in some cases, try stretching yourself a little bit further than might normally feel comfortable. Anyone can – and should be able to – produce a clear, well-written CV.

Why action words matter

The most important words in your CV will be your action words. This is partly because all examples in your Employment section should begin with action words, and partly because these are the words that show employers what you are capable of **doing**.

You may not believe it yet but how you describe what you do can give someone a strong impression of the kind of person you are. They might even assume you have certain character traits.

The following examples show how the action word you choose can make a big difference:

1 'On your first day in your new job, you walked towards the building, looking up at the company name above the door.'

This is a simple, straightforward description of what you did. Nothing wrong with it, but it says very little about you as a person.

2 'On your first day in your new job, you strolled towards the building, glancing up at the company name above the door.'

This choice of words suggests a much more casual approach. Strolling and glancing implies a person who was relaxed, and not fazed – but possibly not very enthusiastic either.

3 'On your first day in your new job, you crept towards the building, peeking up at the company name above the door.'

You sound like a timid, nervous person who was scared about starting work.

4 'On your first day in your new job, you raced towards the building, checking the company name above the door.'

Hmmm ... overslept?

5 'On your first day in your new job, you marched towards the building, gazing up at the company name above the door.'

This suggests a more purposeful approach; that you were feeling confident and looking forward to your new role.

All five sentences, essentially, say the same thing as the first one. However, the impression you are left with of the person described varies enormously, and depends purely on the action words chosen. Exactly the same process will be at work in the mind of the person reading your CV. How you describe what you've done – or what you can do – will make a huge difference to how they perceive you, your abilities, and even your whole attitude to work.

Refining your action words

With this in mind, check your CV factsheet for the skill examples in your Employment section. These bullet points should all have action words at or very near the beginning, which describe what you were doing in that role.

Look carefully at these action words: have you used the best possible one to describe what you did? If it could give the wrong impression about you, think of another way to put it. Most 'standard' action words have one or more 'power' alternatives to try instead.

Finding the right word to use is all about balance. Your CV is, after all, about you. Sometimes you'll feel more comfortable with a straightforward action word than the power alternative, especially if the power alternative is a word you:

- ▶ would never normally say
- ▶ have never used
- ▶ are not comfortable pronouncing
- ▶ feel is a bit too strong to describe what you actually did.

This is absolutely fine: when you turn up at the interview your CV gets you, you won't want it to look as if it were written by someone else.

Power action words

On the other hand, there is nothing wrong with making the very most of everything you've done; in many cases, there is more than one alternative you can consider. The following list might spark some ideas:

Examples

| Basic | Coming up with a business plan |
| | Writing a business plan |

There is nothing wrong with coming up with good ideas, although it can suggest it was a bit of a spur of the moment thing. If all you did was write it, does that mean someone else told you what to put?

Power alternatives	Building a business plan
	Creating a business plan
	Devising a business plan

Built it from scratch, created something, devised something brilliant ... all these sound more impressive and more personally responsible for the outcome.

| Basic | Changing a system |

This doesn't mention whether things were better after your change ... or even whether the change was deliberate.

Power alternatives	Improving a system
	Overhauling an entire system
	Upgrading a system

You improved one or more aspects, overhauled the whole thing, upgraded to a better version ... all these alternatives suggest a much more positive action and result.

| Basic | Answering the telephone |

(Contd)

So ... do you put it down again without saying a word? HOW do you answer it?

| Power alternatives | Representing the company by answering all incoming calls |
| | Creating a positive first impression for all callers |

If you work on reception or switchboard and put external calls through, using words like these can show that you realize how important a good first impression can be to a company's reputation.

If you do something as a result of answering the telephone, focus on what you do:

Power alternatives	Dealing with customer enquiries
	Handling customer enquiries
	Resolving customer enquiries

These suggest you are actively taking charge of your telephone calls and make you sound more like a problem solver.

| Basic | Agreeing the budget |

Put this way, you may have done nothing more than say 'Ok, yes' to a budget.

Power alternatives	Planning the budget
	Setting the budget
	Determining the budget
	Negotiating the budget

These describe a person who is actively involved in what goes into this budget and the level at which it is fixed.

| Basic | Keeping to the budget |

Working within budget limits is a useful skill but can sound very passive.

Power alternatives   <u>Controlling</u> the budget
<u>Managing</u> the budget
<u>Completing</u> an action/project within budget

Taking control of a budget, managing all aspects of it, or achieving something without overspending, all put your actions in a better, more powerful context.

Basic   <u>Serving</u> customers in a shop

Power alternatives   <u>Assisting</u> customers with their purchases
<u>Advising</u> customers about product features
<u>Selling</u> products to customers on commission
<u>Recommending</u> items to complement existing purchases
<u>Promoting</u> sale items and offers to customers at the till

Assisting or advising someone suggests taking a more active part in selling a customer something, rather than simply taking their money for a purchase they decided on all by themselves. Words like selling, promoting or recommending are even more active and therefore powerful.

Basic   <u>Stacking</u> shelves

Power alternatives   <u>Arranging</u> products on shelf clearly and attractively
<u>Merchandising</u> products accurately according to planogram

(Contd)

<u>Avoiding</u> out of stocks
<u>Increasing</u> sales by avoiding
gaps on shelves

Stacking shelves, in itself, suggests a physical activity that requires no thought. The alternatives indicate that you understand why this job is an important one to the company's success, or focuses on a particular aspect that requires more thought, such as accurately following a planogram (a map of where each product is supposed to sit).

The last two examples are best as the action in each case describes a direct benefit to the employer.

Basic	<u>In charge</u> of the top sales team
Power alternatives	<u>Co-ordinating</u> the top sales team
	<u>Building</u> the top sales team
	<u>Managing</u> the top sales team
	<u>Leading</u> the top sales team
	<u>Motivating</u> the top sales team
	<u>Inspiring</u> the top sales team

Being put in charge of something doesn't mean you have contributed to its success or will do in the future. The meaning of each power verb differs, suggesting a different type of involvement. They also imply you directly affected the end result: the fact that this sales team is top.

Choose the word which best shows the type of skill you want to demonstrate. Co-ordinating isn't as powerful as building, managing or leading a team, while motivating and inspiring are skills that the very best managers display.

Never use the term 'trying to' when describing something you worked on. Even if you weren't given time to finish the job or weren't able to for reasons beyond your control, it suggests you couldn't achieve something. This kind of example is not a strong one.

If you didn't finish a task, choose an aspect of it that you did finish – or focus on how your contribution supported the person or team that did complete the task.

Present vs. past tense

For your action verbs you can use one of two tenses:

- ▶ Doing (present tense)
- ▶ Did (past tense)

It's up to you which you use.

One school of thought advises keeping all verbs/action words in the present tense, even when describing jobs or achievements from your past. The present tense can make older skills and examples sound more current, helping your entire CV to feel more dynamic. (You may have noticed that all the power verb alternatives are written in the present tense.)

However, another school of thought favours the past tense. The reasoning behind this is that writing:

- ▶ **Devising** innovative business plans

instead of

- ▶ **Devised** innovative business plans

could suggest to some people that you haven't yet developed that particular skill and are still working on it, instead of having mastered it successfully.

Some readers of your CV may have a strong preference one way or the other; others won't take much notice and will only be concerned which action words you use. If a recruitment agent rewrites your CV into the other tense to suit their house style, it doesn't mean that you were wrong – just that they or their company have certain preferences.

Both approaches are equally valid: select whichever tense you feel most comfortable using. But take care to stick to the tense you choose – and double check it stays the same throughout your CV. Consistency is essential.

Refining your adjectives

Adjectives, or description words, are another way to turn a standard role or activity into something special. They are also useful for refining your CV profile.

Power adjectives, when used properly, describe your position or achievement in a concrete way. They help the reader to compare you positively against other people who appear to have a similar history to your own.

Example

Let's say you are in sales and up against hundreds of other salespeople for the job of account manager at another company. Describing yourself as 'leader of a sales team' won't make you stand out from this crowd. It could be any sales team you're talking about – maybe even the worst one in the country.

Better, you could be ...
- leading an **award-winning** sales team
- contributing to the most **successful** sales team ever
- the **fastest** closer in the telesales team
- the third **highest grossing** salesperson in the division
- voted **top** salesperson by the Sales and Marketing department three years running
- the second most **successful** salesman of 2008
- the **only** account manager **never to have lost a customer**
- the **leading** commission earner in the sales department
- the **first** to make a sale in the on licence sector.

You'll notice that these adjectives (in bold) are not only positive but specific and measurable. This indicates that what you are saying has substance. Even if you don't say in your CV what award your 'award-winning team' managed to achieve, the mere mention of it invites someone to interview you and find out more.

Another way to achieve the same effect and make it clear that you can back up your claim with evidence is to talk about yourself using the following kinds of phrases:

- '**proven** negotiator'
- '**strong track record** in selling to retail'
- '**renowned** public speaker'
- '**demonstrable** communication skills'
- '**recognized** leader'
- '**award-winning** designer'

All of these expressions say to the reader that solid proof of your claims exists. It might be somewhere else in your CV, something you could explain or provide if asked at interview, or something a professional reference from your former employer would back up. However you supply the proof, referring to it in a specific and measurable way adds a great deal of power to your CV.

Use your power carefully

Try not to overuse power words. Too many and the reader may
switch off completely. If you claim to be a motivated, articulate,
committed, innovative, intelligent, charismatic, service-oriented
retail manager, the person reading your CV probably will have
stopped believing in you long before they even find out that you
work in retail.

Use power where it counts

Use power words appropriately. Describe yourself in ways that
are relevant to the work you want. Be wary of claiming to be
an articulate, intelligent, analytical, commercially aware person
if you're applying for work as a silver service waitress. Most
prospective employers would assume without even reading the rest
of your CV that you are overqualified and therefore unlikely to
stay in the job for long.

Avoid repetition

Power words quickly lose their strength and impact if they are repeated too often. Just as friends you know may have particular catchphrases that they like to use, so is it easy to fall into the trap of using the same adjectives to describe everything you do.

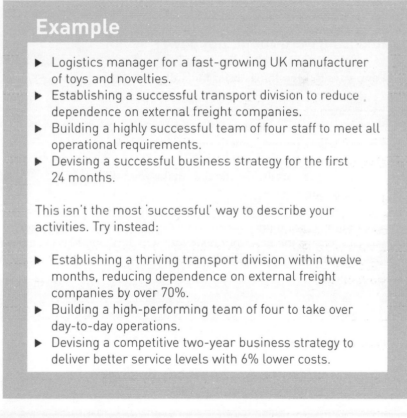

Example

- ▶ Logistics manager for a fast-growing UK manufacturer of toys and novelties.
- ▶ Establishing a successful transport division to reduce dependence on external freight companies.
- ▶ Building a highly successful team of four staff to meet all operational requirements.
- ▶ Devising a successful business strategy for the first 24 months.

This isn't the most 'successful' way to describe your activities. Try instead:

- ▶ Establishing a thriving transport division within twelve months, reducing dependence on external freight companies by over 70%.
- ▶ Building a high-performing team of four to take over day-to-day operations.
- ▶ Devising a competitive two-year business strategy to deliver better service levels with 6% lower costs.

By varying the words that you use, you help to give all your adjectives more power.

If you are using Microsoft Word, a quick way to check whether you are guilty of excessive repetition in your CV is to click on

'Edit' and then 'Find'. Type your favourite power adjective into the box and see how many times it features in your CV. More than twice and you need to start thinking of other ways to say what you mean.

A thesaurus, either online or hard copy, can be useful if you run out of ways to say something.

Reducing word count, not power

Four ways to keep things brief but still powerful include:

- ▶ writing in note form, not full sentences
- ▶ avoiding repeating words and phrases
- ▶ not telling people something they already know (or can safely assume)
- ▶ keeping in specific details that make your skills stand out.

The following example uses all these points together to show how you can refine a job description step by step until you have a concise demonstration of your ability.

Examples

Example 1

Sales Representative, Southern Region, ABC Medical Equipment Ltd

My main duties included selling medical equipment across the southern region. I was responsible for booking equipment demonstrations and trials with doctors and nurses. My monthly sales target was to sell ten every month.

Rule A: use bullets.

Don't waste words writing in full sentences: bullet points are more concise.

Don't repeat words unnecessarily: equipment is mentioned twice in the first sentence, while monthly is referred to twice in the last.

Example 1a

Sales Representative, Southern Region, ABC Medical Equipment Ltd

- ▶ Duties included selling medical equipment across southern region.
- ▶ Responsible for giving demonstrations and trials to medical staff.
- ▶ Sales target ten per month.

Rule B: don't mention unspoken/assumed things.

Don't bother with phrases like 'responsible for' or 'duties included' – just put what you did, beginning each sentence with a verb/action word. The reader knows what you are referring to.

Example 1b

Sales Representative, Southern Region, ABC Medical Equipment Ltd

- ▶ Selling medical equipment across southern region.
- ▶ Giving demonstrations and trials to medical staff.
- ▶ Targeted to sell ten per month.

Rule C: drop unnecessary detail.

Leave out the area you covered: it isn't as important as your skills. If region matters as you can bring existing contacts to your new role, it's already mentioned in your job title.

(Contd)

'Medical equipment' can be dropped for the same reason. The first bullet then becomes 'Selling', which should be obvious for a salesperson!

Trials/demonstrations explain what you do but also apply to any salesperson selling equipment. However, who you sell to, i.e. medical staff and not wholesalers or purchasing managers, is relevant and worth keeping in.

The sales target is specific, but meaningless outside the company. Is this a challenging or an easy target? Did you meet it? Turn this point into an achievement, or delete it.

Example 1c

Sales Representative, Southern Region, ABC Medical Equipment Ltd

▶ Selling to medical staff

Not much left now, is there? So ...

Rule D: include relevant details

You need to keep your word count low; you also need enough relevant details to help an employer decide whether to interview you. Useful information might be:

What you sell: low cost high volume, high cost low volume, technical, disposable?

Who you sell to: GPs, hospitals, pharmacies, business managers, NHS supply?

The channels you sell to: Private, NHS, direct vs. wholesale?

This gives a far better idea how well you are likely to understand the product, target market, and decision-making/buying process.

Also relevant are the skills you use/show when doing your day-to-day activities, rather than simply stating the activities (giving demos and trials).

Example 1d

▶ **Selling** high value oxygen monitors to the private sector and NHS.
▶ **Working** with nurses, consultants and paramedics.
▶ **Demonstrating** equipment to medical staff.

At this stage you're including better information, but there's still no real power. It's not specific enough; there's no proof you do a good job. The words themselves may be action words, but they are also weak. To finish your examples off, you need to refine them.

Refining/adding power

The example below takes this one step further by showing how you can refine your points using power alternatives for the action words and making descriptions more specific.

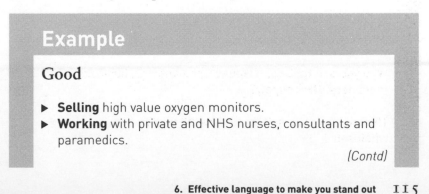

Example

Good

▶ **Selling** high value oxygen monitors.
▶ **Working** with private and NHS nurses, consultants and paramedics.

(Contd)

▶ **Demonstrating** *equipment to medical staff.*

Better

▶ **Selling** new, high value oxygen monitors successfully.
▶ **Forming relationships** with private and NHS nurses, consultants and paramedics.
▶ **Communicating product benefits** while training groups of ten medical staff.

Best

▶ **Beating annual sales target** by 10 per cent in 2009.
▶ **Successfully positioning** new, high value oxygen monitors as essential equipment.
▶ **Building lasting relationships** with private/NHS consultants, paramedics and nurses.
▶ **Reinforcing product benefits** while single-handedly training staff in groups of ten.

TEN THINGS TO REMEMBER

1 *The language you choose is very important.*

2 *Refining your words will add power to your CV.*

3 *The first words you read make the biggest impact.*

4 *Make action words the basis of your CV.*

5 *Always think about power alternatives for action words.*

6 *Proof should remain at the heart of your CV.*

7 *Justified use of adjectives can add value.*

8 *Empty descriptions and 'management speak' don't add instant value.*

9 *You can refine your language without swallowing a dictionary.*

10 *Keep language you are comfortable with – but stretch yourself a little.*

7

True lies: when marketing becomes deceit

In this chapter you will:
* **define a lie**
* **appreciate the risks of lying on your CV**

However well you present your skills and achievements in a positive light, there will probably still be areas of your CV where you wish you had something better to say. It can be very tempting, when looking at these less impressive parts of your CV, to make something up. But the only possible advice for someone in this situation is: **Don't**.

Education lies

Let's say you lie about your grades or qualifications. They don't quite meet the job spec or aren't something you feel proud of. What happens when you are asked for evidence? Where would a certificate come from … or could you sit a test to prove your knowledge?

Lies are not just when you claim to have something that you don't – exaggeration is also a form of lying. You don't feel proud of your 2.2 in English from Bristol University so you bump it up – just a little – to a 2.1. Or maybe you say you got your degree from Cambridge University instead, as you had a girlfriend there.

How could you possibly be found out? Lots of ways:

▶ An interviewer who studied English at Cambridge themselves and wants to know which tutor you had.
▶ A chance search on Facebook, where you clearly show as part of the Bristol University network.
▶ A pre- (or post-) interview screening by a professional screening company in which your university attendance and results are verified.

Employment lies

When you lie about a former job or exaggerate your responsibilities, what happens when your prospective employer ... contacts your old boss? ... Googles you and finds an old web page showing your real job title? ... asks the professional screening company to make a few calls?

Other lies

There may be some areas of your CV where you think you are quite safe to lie. Little lies, because you can't possibly get caught – not even by the professionals. A more interesting-sounding interest; elevating your spoken Spanish from tourist to business level; several months' travel abroad to cover up that inconvenient gap in your employment.

If an untruthful CV does get you to interview, can you carry through your lies convincingly? You could be challenged in any number of ways, not just at interview but in future:

▶ You add yoga as an interest: your interviewer turns out to be a Hatha Yoga instructor.
▶ You claim advanced spoken German: the HR manager spent a year in the Munich branch (or married a German) and happens to speak it fluently.
▶ You add 'six months' backpacking in Vietnam', thinking it an unusual destination, but end up face to face with someone who toured South East Asia during their gap year.
▶ You mention abseiling as a hobby, but then refuse to go near a climbing wall during your first corporate event, citing your lifelong fear of heights.

What's the worst that can happen?

If you do decide to go the untruthful route, you will have to see it through to the end, one way or another. Frequently, the end is not good.

Not everyone can be a Lee McQueen, the winning contestant on the 2008 series of BBC TV's *The Apprentice*. McQueen lied about his education on his CV, got caught out during an interview, and yet *still* got the job. The boardroom explanation for this unusual decision was that McQueen was believed to have lied simply because he wanted the job so much – and that this level of eagerness was actually a positive thing. In fact, most employers do not appreciate this kind of eagerness; they prefer integrity.

Being caught in one lie, even if it is a 'small' one, will cast doubt on everything else that you claim in your CV. If it really is that small a lie, why bother with it, especially if it could cancel out all the genuine skills you offer?

Lying on your CV to get a job is considered by most employers to be gross misconduct. This can lead to instant dismissal, whether they find out about the lie on day 1 or day 1000 of your new job.

When does a stretch become a lie?

Only you know when a slight exaggeration of your skills and abilities tips the scales and becomes a lie. If your moral compass tells you that you're pushing it, or the thought of being challenged or asked for detail makes you at all nervous, don't put it in your CV.

Feedback suggests that when companies specify in their job adverts that all applications will go through a screening process to verify accuracy, the number of applicants falls by around 15 per cent. That would suggest at least 1 in 7 people are very worried about something they've written in their CV. Many employers use screening without informing applicants, so it's best to play safe.

What if I'm just not good enough?

As a rule, always apply for jobs you are qualified and competent to do. However, that doesn't mean you should assume you aren't good enough or that an employer won't consider you for a particular job just because you don't meet every single one of their requirements. There is usually a mix of essential and nice-to-have skills listed on any job advert. Provided you meet the essential requirements, don't be put off if you don't have every nice-to-have skill or quite as many years of experience as they are asking. If you want to operate on sick patients you obviously need surgical qualifications but for many jobs you can often succeed by selling the skills and experience you do have because an employer may still appreciate what you can offer.

As long as you are being realistic about your ability to do the job in question, it's worth applying. There is more on this in Part four, Targeting it carefully.

Do I have to be honest about everything?

Every claim you make in your CV must be truthful. However, there is no rule that says you have to mention absolutely everything.

There are some things that, if you would rather not share them on your CV, you are perfectly entitled to leave out. This is not lying: it's being selective with information in order to present yourself in the best possible light.

'Spent' convictions, for example, do not have to be declared to a prospective employer. However, if your sentence was long enough to leave a noticeable gap in your employment, concealing this fact can be difficult.

If you think your interests are really boring – or bizarre – and it makes you feel uncomfortable to include them, then don't. You can simply leave the Interests section out. That's not to say you won't be asked about your Interests at interview, but it might help you get invited to one in the first place.

Some omissions will arouse suspicion. Unexplained gaps in employment are rarely ignored. Glaring omissions will result in detailed questions at interview (best case) or could just mean your CV gets junked right from the start (worst case), so you will need to find a way to handle these.

If I can't lie, what can I do?

Taking the honest approach doesn't mean all your warts
have to be on display. Most problem areas can be successfully
dealt with by what can be called 'honest spin'. This is covered in
Chapter 8.

TEN THINGS TO REMEMBER

1 *Don't fabricate anything on your CV.*

2 *Don't 'bump up' grades or qualifications.*

3 *Don't alter dates or other employment details.*

4 *Don't exaggerate the role you played in something.*

5 *Don't force yourself to lie by applying for unrealistic jobs.*

6 *Do be honest with yourself.*

7 *Do stay honest throughout your CV.*

8 *Do check details to ensure you don't lie by mistake.*

9 *Do consider omitting things if you need to.*

10 *Do remember that many applications are screened.*

8

Honest spin: handling problem areas

In this chapter you will:
- *understand the difference between honest spin and lying*
- *construct a positive story or explanation for something*
- *deal with trouble spots using spin*

Just as Max Clifford does for his clients through clever PR, being careful with your words can help transform a lacklustre CV into something everyone wants to read.

The trick is to find a way to make people focus on what *you* want them to focus on.

Generally speaking, it's best not to bring up a problem area if it can be avoided: you are perfectly entitled to be picky about what you include in your CV. Some things will need explanation though, or your reader could end up making assumptions that are much worse than reality. For this, you can use honest spin.

Honest spin doesn't lie about an issue; instead it acknowledges it but focuses on the positive. So, what kind of problems can be tackled using honest spin?

Gaps in employment

Employment gaps can happen to anyone, and can be caused by a number of things:

- ▶ voluntary or involuntary redundancy
- ▶ sabbatical
- ▶ long-term illness
- ▶ being fired
- ▶ career break to raise a family or care for a relative
- ▶ retraining
- ▶ being a school leaver or university graduate
- ▶ a prison sentence
- ▶ travel
- ▶ resigning after making a poor career move.

Any of the above can see you out of work for some time. While many do not actually reflect on your ability to do a job, most employers still see being out of work as negative.

Mind the gap

Shorter gaps of a few weeks or months can sometimes be smoothed over by mentioning only the years (not the years and months) that you worked for an employer. It's an effective way to avoid focusing on any gaps, but because of this some recruiters may automatically view with suspicion any CV that gives only the years of employment.

Longer gaps, or gaps that happen to span two calendar years, tend to look more obvious and it's rather awkward to handle them this way.

Depending on the reason for the gap, it is often better to include a brief explanation rather than leave the reader to fill in the blanks themselves. Chances are you can explain the reasons better and more positively than their imagination will. Volunteering a brief explanation for an employment gap can make you seem a more attractive prospect as it shows you are honest, which sensible employers value highly.

Another way to distract recruiters from a gap is to change the format of your CV so that your skills examples are given before your employment history and dates. This is called a functional CV and will be covered in more detail in Part four, Targeting it carefully.

In the following examples, only the job dates, titles and companies are listed for simplicity.

Handling short gaps

Dec 2008–present	Store Manager, Shoppers Paradise Ltd
Oct 2007–Nov 2008	Deputy Store Manager, Better Retail Group Ltd
Jan 2006–Aug 2007	Assistant Store Manager, Great British Stores Ltd

The two-month gap during 2007 could raise questions in a recruiter's mind, although there is an obvious progression through each job. As it's a short gap, you could try using years only instead:

2008–present	Store Manager, Shoppers Paradise Ltd
2007–2008	Deputy Store Manager, Better Retail Group Ltd
2006–2007	Assistant Store Manager, Great British Stores Ltd

Alternatively, keep the dates complete but give an explanation:

| Dec 2008–present | Store Manager, Shoppers Paradise Ltd |
| Oct 2007–Nov 2008 | Deputy Store Manager, Better Retail Group Ltd |

(Contd)

Aug 2007–Oct 2007	Relocation at short notice due to illness in the family
Jan 2006–Aug 2007	Assistant Store Manager, Great British Stores Ltd

Handling longer gaps

Jan 2008–present	Machinist, Tooltime Ltd
May 2007–Jan 2008	Machinist, Tools Gold Ltd
Oct 2005–Oct 2006	Apprentice Machinist, Tooling Around Ltd

This gap is six months, but stretches across two calendar years.

2008–present	Machinist, Tooltime Ltd
2007–2008	Machinist, Tools Gold Ltd
2005–2006	Apprentice Machinist, Tooling Around Ltd

With only the years given, a reader could assume your gap runs from early 2006 to late 2007: almost two years, instead of six just months. Keeping the gap and explaining it is better:

Jan 2008–present	Machinist, Tooltime Ltd.
May 2007–Jan 2008	Machinist, Tools Gold Ltd
Oct 2006–May 2007	Workforce made redundant and offer of permanent job withdrawn when Tooling Around went into receivership. Relocated to Leicester for full-time job.
Oct 2005–Oct 2006	Apprentice Machinist, Tooling Around Ltd

Temporary employment

Having gaps in between work and jumping around from company to company is par for the course if you do temporary work. This doesn't automatically reflect badly upon you, and some employers value the kind of experience and skills this type of work can bring.

To avoid someone making the wrong assumption, it can be worth adding a couple of lines to introduce your temp status before getting into dates.

Example

Range of office-based temporary administration positions gained through two principal agencies. Always in demand and often requested for repeat assignments.

▶ Devising new admin processes to bring order to chaos in short-staffed offices.
▶ Saving Filing Fantasies seven man hours per week after completing one-month project.
▶ Initiating weekly management reports and automated downloads from SAP.
▶ Enabling Kinells to reduce overall stock levels by 28 per cent.
▶ Providing effective short-term cover for a broad range of roles at short notice.
▶ Recognized by all five employers for flexibility, fast learning and creative problem solving.

Jun 2009–Jan 2010	Administration Clerk (maternity cover), Filing Fantasies
May 2009	SAP Reporting Assistant, Green's Gardenware Ltd
Feb 2009–Apr 2009	Administration Assistant, Filing Fantasies

(Contd)

Dec 2008–Jan 2009	Purchase Ledger Clerk, Forking Flowers Ltd
Oct 2008–Nov 2008	Accounts Assistant, Kinells Distribution Ltd
Sep 2008	Stock Control Clerk, Green's Gardenware Ltd
Aug 2008	Personal Assistant, Filing Fantasies
Jul 2008–Aug 2008	Accounts Assistant, Legal Eagles Recruitment

The biggest challenge with long periods of temporary work is making sure you don't include excessive detail: it is very easy to become repetitious, especially if you are doing similar roles for each employer.

If you have done temp work for a long time or for a lot of different employers, you can group your employers, skills and achievements to make clearer what you have to offer:

Example

Jan–Dec 2009	Various financial administration roles for large companies: Nostromo Shipbuilders, Cerne Abbas Holdings, H. Solo Enterprises, and The Dish & Spoon Company Ltd.

► Controlling spend by setting up SAP approval routes to validate purchase orders.
► Training all staff on SAP, including Power Users to field queries when placement over.
► Saving man hours and supporting management by creating automated reporting.
► Enabling non-SAP users to control budgets by devising spreadsheets for shared use.

Brief employment

We all make mistakes from time to time; careers are no exception. This section refers to permanent jobs that for some reason end up being short-lived, rather than temporary jobs that are intentionally short.

Sometimes a new permanent job can last as little as a few days or weeks – especially if it turns out not as you expected, hoped or were promised. A job guaranteeing support that never materializes; a clash of personalities with new management; an unpleasant company culture or unethical working practices; there are many reasons why you might come to regret taking a particular job and need to move on quickly.

If you can find alternative work fast, and can do so without leaving a gap on your CV, that's great. Depending on the amount of time you were in the job, you may then decide whether to mention it.

Examples

1 You spend one week in a new commission-only sales job before realizing the earnings guarantees were pure fantasy. You find something else straight away and move on.

You can leave this out of your CV. It won't affect your dates of employment, even when given in months, and doesn't impact the skills and abilities you can offer an employer.

2 You move to a new job and, after realizing it's a huge mistake, are lucky enough to get your old job back again within the month. You didn't burn your bridges when you left, and your old employer is happy to save the cost of recruiting your replacement.

Again, you can leave this out of your CV to avoid lengthy explanations at this stage.

While leaving information out of your CV is not lying, it doesn't mean you can forget about it or pretend it never happened. If at interview you are asked directly whether you have ever made a bad job move, or have ever spent time out of work, then you should answer honestly.

Be prepared to explain your past in a positive light. By all means say that you left it off your CV because you didn't feel it added anything to your capabilities. By giving it proper thought beforehand, it won't come as such a shock to be asked the question – and you won't be tempted to try to lie when put on the spot.

How to use honest SPIN

When explaining something on your CV, from employment gaps to unfinished courses, it helps to follow a few simple rules. Keep it:

▶ Short
▶ Positive
▶ Informative
▶ Natural.

SHORT

Don't take pages to give every last detail of your situation. Stay brief and to the point.

POSITIVE

Think about how you can make this potential 'problem' sound like a good thing. If that's not possible, try to:

▶ Make it appear neutral instead of detrimental.
▶ Point out that it does not diminish what you can offer an employer.
▶ Demonstrate skills gained or opportunities taken as a result.

INFORMATIVE

While keeping it short, do ensure you include any details necessary to avoid confusion.

NATURAL

If this is the first time you have tried to explain something in a positive light, make sure you feel comfortable with it and that it will hold up under scrutiny. Your explanation should feel natural, and you need to be convincing when discussing it. If you don't believe it, no one else will.

The four rules of honest **SPIN** apply to any explanation you may give, whether in an application form, a covering letter or even at interview.

Work on your 'story'

The following exercise can be a great way to think through any problem areas prior to interview, whether you mention them on your CV or during the application process or not.

Problem 1: Taking a long time to find your first job

When you left college you didn't really know what you wanted to do, and it was a few months before research helped you learn enough to apply for jobs you wanted. Meantime you made ends meet with factory work. You finally got a perfect job in the January, having been shortlisted from 25 applicants, and you have enjoyed it for two years since then.

(Contd)

You are now applying for your next job on this career path, and worry that this initial delay in finding work will look bad on your CV. You can't put years instead of months to hide the gap, because you started the job in a new year. Listing your factory work fills the gap in your Employment History, but it is irrelevant and 'beneath' the career you are now following. You aren't sure if you want to mention it at all. What should you do?

The first step is to believe in yourself. List some of the positive actions you took:

1 You researched careers until you found the right one for you.

Research is a skill in itself. You didn't just wait for a job to fall into your lap. (If you did to start with, don't admit it!) See yourself as determined, prepared to wait for the right role. Employers like people who know what they want: they are more likely to stay in their job.

2 You worked another job while you did your research.

This shows willingness to work, time management, and motivation. You could argue that you took 'lesser' factory (or bar, or warehouse, or temp) work because it left you freer to conduct research, phone employers, write applications and attend interviews.

3 You had lots of interviews before landing the job you wanted.

Lots of interviews suggests you have skills or qualifications that employers want. There's nothing wrong with taking your time to find the right employer and role; with your first job, it's just a bit more obvious how long this stage takes.

Good

When I left college I wasn't quite sure what I wanted to do, so I spent a few months working nights and looking into many different types of job. I decided I'd be best suited to office work but once I started applying, it took a long time to attend all the interviews and so it was a few weeks before I landed the right one.

Reasonable. Honest but waffly and non-specific, so it sounds a bit like an excuse.

Better

After leaving college I worked nights as a warehouse operative so I could research lots of different careers. Administration appealed the most and after applying I was invited to many interviews. I landed my dream job, with a company I still enjoy working for.

This is better as it is shorter, more positive, more informative, but still feels natural. There is lots of obvious information and not enough selling of your skills though.

Best

While working nights I researched career options through my local library and contacts. It became clear that my numeracy, organization and IT skills were perfectly suited to administration and it was worth the wait, as I beat 24 other candidates to land my first job.

This makes the whole 'ordeal' sound like it was planned, enjoyable, and effective – while also pointing out your core skills and how many people you beat to land your current job. The length hasn't increased but it is more informative, while still sounding natural.

Then try writing out your first explanation, clearly and honestly, remembering the above.

This final 'story' should be the basis of your CV entry. Working while researching your career is more positive than doing nothing, so do include your factory job in your CV:

Jul 2009–Jan 2010   **Warehouse Operative, Gorgeous Gateaux Ltd**

▶ Handling inbound/outbound goods within strict deadlines on night shift while investigating potential careers by day.
▶ Developing my research skills using the Internet, libraries and personal contacts.
▶ Beating 24 other candidates to land my dream job in administration based on my organization and IT skills.

Once you have a couple more years' experience under your belt, it's unlikely you'll need to put any detail against this job at all. Employers will be far more interested in what you've done in your career since, and what you can offer them.

Work on your positive story

Problem 2: An employment gap after redundancy

You were made redundant at very short notice along with 30 colleagues when your struggling employer had to shut down an entire division. The redundancy came as a surprise to all of you, but it took almost nine months to find your next role. How do you explain this big a gap in a positive way?

The answers to these three points are the basis of your explanation.

1 Redundancy is about luck – bad luck – and not about skill. It can hit anyone at any time and if you're really unlucky, more than once. But it's important to see – and believe – that being made redundant is no reflection on your skills or abilities. (Unless of course, like Nick Leeson, you were the reason for your last employer's downfall, in which case your CV is probably the least of your worries right now.)

2 If you were made redundant suddenly, it can be easier to justify a longer gap as you had no time to start a job search before leaving. If you took voluntary redundancy or had plenty of warning, how quickly did you jump into action, or did you do something else before focusing on your job search? What did you do, and did this gain you any skills?

3 In general, what have you done while unemployed? Learned any new skills? Done any training courses, voluntary or charity work, computer courses, learned a language, started your own business, coached a junior football team, renovated your house? Focus on the routine you've kept, activities you've done, what you've learned and what you can offer, not on the fact you weren't in paid work.

Good

After being made redundant at short notice, I worked as a community volunteer while searching for a new job. I volunteered almost immediately as I wanted to do something different, to work with people instead of systems. Being a specialist, it took several months to find an equivalent role but eventually I was lucky.

Honest and natural, but too much focus on being out of work and your luck at finding a new job: suggests events were beyond your control. Not enough emphasis on what you gained from the experience.

Better

Following redundancy at short notice, I wanted to improve my skills while looking for work. Volunteering seemed a good way to do this
(Contd)

and I focused on roles that involved working closely with people rather than systems. This experience improved my interpersonal skills.

Still honest and natural but now more specific about what you set out to achieve while out of work – and preferably even briefer.

Best

Following redundancy I wanted to broaden my skills while planning my next career move. Working closely with people as a volunteer fundraiser improved my interpersonal and communication skills while helping to raise more than £25,000 in just nine months.

This almost suggests that this hiatus was voluntary – that you were planning your next career move rather than unwillingly spending time out of work. Although unpaid you still excelled in your role and benefited the organization, developing useful skills on the way.

Now you're thinking positively, the entry on your CV could look like this:

Jan 2007–Nov 2007   **Volunteer Fundraising and Events Co-ordinator, RSPU**

- ▶ Focusing on enhancing interpersonal and communication skills after redundancy.
- ▶ Raising more than £25,000 in just nine months with a team of three volunteers.
- ▶ Building a network of relationships with local businesspeople to raise the charity's profile.
- ▶ Organizing events such as a memorable three-legged 'horse' race through the town centre.

If you didn't do any kind of work but did training instead, focus on what you've learned in the same way:

Jan 2007–Nov 2007   Skills development

▶ Broadening my computing, financial and language skills following redundancy.
▶ Gaining CLAIT qualification, experience setting up macro-based Excel reporting.
▶ Enhancing budget management skills by studying accounting and bookkeeping.
▶ Learning to speak Spanish as a Foreign Language – awarded Elementary certificate.

Insight

Never mention or try to explain issues with previous employers on your CV.

▶ Don't give a reason for leaving.
▶ Don't say if you were fired.
▶ Don't criticize a former employer.
▶ Don't mention an employment tribunal you were involved in.

Reason for leaving

Your CV is simply not the place to discuss your reasons for leaving. If these do need to be addressed, do it at interview – indeed it is quite common to be questioned on why you changed roles or why you are looking for a job now – but don't give the information up front. It won't add to your appeal, especially if you were fired.

Employer criticism

If you bad mouth a former employer (even if it is wholly justified in your view), it can suggest that you are a difficult personality. A reader could see you as a complainer, someone who will fall out with your next employer – and possibly end up talking about them negatively as well.

The same applies to interviews – if you've had problems with an employer, find a way to describe them diplomatically and move on to the more positive aspects.

Employment tribunals

Don't mention tribunals unless asked. However justified, and however successful the result, you may still come across as the kind of person prepared to fight your employer through legal proceedings – something that many employers are understandably wary of.

If you do have to tackle the subject, do it at interview and discuss the facts calmly and positively. Focus on what you can offer an employer and what you look for in an ideal role, rather than on what hasn't worked in the past or what you don't like.

Rehabilitation of offenders

Problem 3: Prison

I was in prison for 18 months after being convicted of dangerous driving. It has left a noticeable gap in my employment history. How do I get around this on my CV?

If your CV gap is due to a spell at Her Majesty's Pleasure, this can be a little more thorny.

Most employers view even rehabilitated offenders with caution, so it is understandable if you don't wish to reveal this information.

However, it's not all doom and gloom; the Rehabilitation of Offenders Act (1974) may help if your sentence was some time ago.

If you were convicted of a criminal offence with a sentence (whether a suspended sentence or time spent in prison) of two and a half years or less, and you do not re-offend within the typical rehabilitation period of ten years, then your conviction becomes officially 'spent'. The rehabilitation period can be as short as five years for a young offender who was under 18 when convicted.

Under current legislation, a sentence of more than two and a half years can never be 'spent'.

For many types of job, you are not obliged to give any details of a 'spent' conviction to a prospective employer; you don't even have to admit its existence. However, there are exceptions if you apply to work with vulnerable people: children, the elderly, or the sick. In these cases you must reveal all convictions, whether spent or not.

Concealing a spent conviction

If you wish to conceal a spent conviction that creates a gap of more than a few months in your Employment History, and you are not applying to work with vulnerable people, you have three choices:

1 Leave an unexplained employment gap: be prepared that this could result in your CV being binned, or (best case) that you'll need to answer interview questions to explain the gap. You could feasibly say you were unemployed (which you effectively were) and unable to find work during that time (which is effectively true).

2 Fill the gap – with honesty, focused on the positives. If while in prison you did any of the following or learned anything that could be considered beneficial to a future employer, focus on this:

  ▷ took any courses
  ▷ retrained
  ▷ developed any new skills
  ▷ wrote a book
  ▷ learned a language
  ▷ did a job.

Just as you would with a period of unemployment on your CV, list the skills and experiences you gained during that time as your 'positive sell'.

3 If you feel you have no option but to lie outright, all the concerns of the previous chapter still apply. Checks can and probably will be made, and you may have to answer detailed questions at interview.

Convictions that are not spent

These aren't something you can hide for long, as you will need to inform any prospective employer at some point, but there's nothing that says you have to advertise it on your CV.

You are probably more likely to get to interview if you don't mention it up front. In person is by far the best way to try to explain your past, sell your skills, and convince an employer to take you on. If you conceal something on your CV in order to have a better chance at getting an interview, make sure you put down something simple, not an elaborate fiction. Then, after hopefully making a positive first impression, raise the subject at an early opportunity rather than waiting until a probing question forces you to.

Make it clear to the interviewer why you felt it was better to do this than to be honest. You could say something like 'Honesty is important to me and I had no intention of trying to conceal this fact/issue from you. However, I was hoping for a chance to discuss it face to face rather than on paper so you could ask any questions you need to. As you can see, it doesn't have any bearing on my X, Y and Z skills, or on my integrity as an employee.' (Obviously if you were sentenced for white collar fraud you might need to stop at 'skills'.)

Otherwise, handle your employment gap due to a prison sentence the same as you would for any other reason. Focus on the transferable skills you have learned, and make sure you have a clear, well thought out story about your time out of work that always comes back to what you can offer this employer.

Illness

> ## Problem 4: Long-term illness
>
> Several years ago I was diagnosed with bipolar disorder and was prescribed medication. I stopped taking the medication when I was made redundant and then suffered an acute episode which resulted in three months' hospitalization.
>
> A combination of therapy and new medication settled everything down and I felt back to normal, and was able to find another job through a friend. I'm now looking for my next move. Do I have to mention any of this in my CV, as I spent a total of six months off work?

It's simplest if, by the time of writing your CV, your illness is over and you have completely recovered. If your past illness or current condition won't affect your ability to do this new job – and you have your doctor's agreement on this – it's worth explaining, but very briefly.

Example

Oct 2004–May 2005	**Recovering from illness: pronounced fit 30 April 2005**
Sept 2001–Oct 2004	**Bursar, Dazzlebury School**

This example indicates you are back to full health. If you managed to do anything relevant to an employer during your recovery, mention it here:

Oct 2004–May 2005   Recovering from illness, pronounced fit 30 April 2005

► Learning French via CD: Elementary exam booked for July 2005

Sept 2001–Oct 2004   Bursar, Dazzlebury School

If you went on to another job after your illness, it needs no more explanation than that because it's obvious you are fine to work:

Jun 2005–Apr 2009   Admissions Secretary, Finklethorpe University

► Radically overhauling the admissions system to improve performance measurement.

Oct 2004–May 2005   Recovering from illness

► Learning French via CD: elementary exam passed July 2005.

Sept 2000–Oct 2004   Bursar, Dazzlebury School

► Managing budgets effectively to meet all curriculum development and staffing needs.

> If your illness was very long term or its impact on you is ongoing to some extent, your focus should still be on what you can do, not on what you can't.

Of course the type of job you apply for needs to be appropriate to your circumstances. If you are a qualified mechanic now unable to do physical work, you might not cut it as a mechanic but could bring unparalleled technical knowledge to the role of parts manager, service manager or new car salesman at a dealership. If both you and your doctor are confident you are capable to do this work, you apply for the right role, and you sell your skills in the right way, then you become an attractive prospect despite any illness.

Proof

Nervous about starting work again or feel that employers won't believe you when you say you are capable of doing the job? Consider starting work experience or voluntary work to demonstrate your fitness. Depending on the nature of your illness, this may also be a good way to ease yourself back into full-time work, and could give you some recent skill examples to include in your CV.

Disability

If an illness has left you with a long-term limited ability to do certain tasks, this is effectively a disability. In this case, think carefully about what to disclose on your CV or application and during interview.

Mentioning a disability isn't compulsory. If it isn't obvious, it might be very tempting to keep it quiet. But bear in mind that if you do not warn your employer, and you end up unable to do your job properly because of your disability, you can legally be dismissed for poor performance if your employer isn't aware you are disabled.

When mentioning any disability, your CV focus should still be putting a positive spin on what you are able to do unaided, and what further value you can add if the employer makes reasonable adjustments to support you. Never focus on what you can't do.

General rules for explaining gaps

FOCUS ON BENEFITS

Whatever you did during an employment gap, focus on that rather than on being out of work. Include it as a proper entry in your CV, with associated examples, to show an employer how your skills have improved for their benefit.

FOCUS ON RELEVANCE

If the gap is in your past, and you've successfully held down a job since then, a detailed explanation is less likely to be needed.

If you are still unemployed now, your explanation may need to be a little fuller – if not now, then at interview. It's unfair, but until you land that next job there will always be a question mark as to why you are not in work.

Mind your language

When it comes to honest spin, the language you use is all-important. Words can bring all sorts of images into an employer's mind: make sure these images are positive.

NEGATIVE

▶ Unemployed
▶ Out of work

NEUTRAL

▶ Looking for work
▶ Finding a new job

POSITIVE

▶ Researching jobs
▶ Evaluating alternatives
▶ Considering options
▶ Planning your next move

The more active and in control you can make yourself sound, whatever your situation, the more positive you will appear to an employer.

_____

Looking beyond your CV

There may be some issues that, even if not addressed in your CV, will need to be raised at some point. Don't feel you can just ignore these because you're not including them now.

All a great CV can do is get you into the interview room. After that, it's down to you.

Generally speaking, even the most awkward of issues is usually best discussed face to face, because however awkward you may feel, you can at least make sure you are clearly understood.

Another advantage is that by preparing now to explain issues clearly and positively during interview, you'll feel more comfortable with your 'problem area' and be able to talk about it more easily.

TEN THINGS TO REMEMBER

1 *Smooth over trouble spots, don't lie about them.*

2 *Every problem has a story: write yours positively.*

3 *Refine your story with honest SPIN.*

4 *Short explanations are all a CV needs.*

5 *Focus always on the positive points.*

6 *Be informative enough to reassure but stay relevant.*

7 *Keep explanations natural so your CV feels sincere.*

8 *Honest SPIN can be used on any part of your CV.*

9 *If you leave something out of your CV, still write the story and SPIN it.*

10 *The work you do in this chapter is invaluable preparation for interviews.*

9

....

Jargon: when to include, explain or avoid

In this chapter you will learn how to:
- **define jargon**
- **understand when and how to use jargon**

_____

What is jargon?

Jargon consists of words, brands, acronyms, abbreviations and
expressions with specific meanings. It can be industry-specific,
company-specific, technical or generic and it is almost always used
as a kind of shorthand. Jargon allows you to refer to something
in an agreed way that your colleagues should understand. Most
people use jargon in their everyday speech at work and, while some
jargon is fairly specialized, much is so widely used that it becomes
commonplace.

Whether you enjoy using – or reading – jargon is a very personal
thing. Even if it's something you dislike, it can be tempting to use
lots of jargon in your CV simply because it's a great way to save
space. But at the initial stage of the recruitment process – or at any
stage of it – you have no control over who might read your CV.
It could be a specialist, but it could equally be an HR executive
with little or no understanding of the specific role you are applying
for. So, use jargon as little as possible.

There is plenty of generic 'business' jargon about. You may well have:

- heard of **SMART** objectives
- been told to **KISS**
- said the budget was **TBC**
- listed a **URL**
- sent an email **FYI**
- heard a **step-change** is needed
- **benchmarked** performance
- done some **'blue-sky'** thinking.

How you use jargon when talking to your colleagues is up to you. If it saves time and you know it's helping your audience understand you better, then by all means make yourself a target for buzzword bingo. Whenever you are unsure of your audience, use plain English.

Industry-specific jargon is popular and includes many things, such as:

- Finance: **P&L** (profit and loss), **YOY** (year on year), **Sage** (accounting software)
- Printing: **CMYK** (4 colour print process), **CTP** (computer to plate), **B1** (sheet size)
- Retail: **FSDU** (floor standing display unit), **Plano** (where products should go on shelves).

Within a particular industry, this kind of jargon may be widely accepted – especially if it relates to standard equipment, processes or technical specifications – and may even be seen as a way of showing you are knowledgeable in the field. Use this kind of jargon only when it's essential, widely understood, and won't confuse someone who reads it.

Jargon can also be company-specific:

- **JDE** – in-house customer service system
- **XLOB** – across different lines of business

- **Sekunda** – self-erecting unit
- **Tranzit** – artwork file transfer system.

While your colleagues may understand you perfectly, no one outside your organization will. Avoid using any terms like this on your CV.

Rules for jargon

TAKE THE SAME TONE AS THE EMPLOYER

Boundaries for the amount and type of jargon you can safely use are typically set by the advert for the job you are applying for.

When it includes some jargon, you can fairly safely repeat those terms in your CV; indeed you may need to in order for recruiters or scanners to pick up these key words.

For more plainly worded adverts, try to avoid using any jargon at all or – if you have to use some – give an explanation.

If you are applying speculatively to a company and have no advert to refer to, check their website and any other job vacancies they are advertising to see how much jargon is used in their external communications.

KNOW YOUR AUDIENCE

Addressing your CV to an HR department or a recruitment agency means limit your jargon to essentials only, unless you are using key words from their advert.

If the CV should be sent to the manager of the department you would be working for, greater use of jargon is probably acceptable but ensure it is universally understood.

If you don't know who your CV will be read by, always minimize jargon.

APPLYING WITHIN THE SAME INDUSTRY

For a new role in the same industry, any industry-wide technical jargon will probably be understood by your future employer.

However, remember your CV may start with an HR audience so ensure you don't use any more than you need, and that sentences still make sense to someone who doesn't know the technical terms.

APPLYING TO A NEW INDUSTRY

If you are after a change of direction, chances are the industry you apply to will not know or understand the previous field you worked in. In this case remove all industry jargon or, if not possible, provide an explanation.

This can be particularly relevant for military personnel applying for civilian jobs. The military is famous for its extensive jargon, much of which is essential to understanding. However, it creates a real minefield when it comes to de-jargonizing your CV. It helps if you 'translate' your CV: this means focusing on your transferable skills above everything else, and ensuring your relevant skill examples are carefully described in plain English.

TECHNICAL CONSIDERATIONS (FOR EXAMPLE, IT)

In some fields, use of jargon is almost a prerequisite; IT is one of them. If you don't mention the software or programming jargon appropriate to your level, it may be assumed – rightly or wrongly – that you don't have the knowledge or experience you claim.

However, you still need to pass the understandability test. Even if someone doesn't know the particular acronym you are using, it should at least be possible to figure out that it is software, for example.

BEING CONCISE VS. CLEAR

Yes, jargon can help to keep the word count down. However, this shouldn't be at the expense of getting clear messages across in your CV.

FEEDBACK: THE ACID TEST

When in doubt, ask a colleague in your industry and a friend who is totally unrelated to it to give you feedback on your CV. Ask them to be totally honest and to say any parts they didn't understand. If it makes sense to both of them, you have probably got your jargon balance about right.

Examples

Production Manager advert

Applicants need 10+ years' experience managing packaging production, a detailed overview of the entire process including CAD design and CAD-based tool-making, CTP, litho, screen and stereo print, corrugation (single and mixed flutes), lamination, die-cutting and gluing. Understanding of JIT and adherence to ISO 900123 and BS 3456 essential. Specialist knowledge of pharmaceutical packaging regulations (particularly AcuBraille) an advantage.

Then you could say in your CV:

▶ 11 years managing packaging and corrugate production, leading teams of 80 people.
▶ Controlling CAD product design and CTP, all print types, corrugation and finishing.
▶ Devising innovative process solutions to reduce customer lead times by up to 20%.

(Contd)

- ▶ Successfully implementing ISO 900123 and BS 3456 compliance on three different sites.
- ▶ Introducing Bobst Mistral AcuBraille system for pharmaceutical packaging in 2009.

If the advert had said instead:

Production Manager

Applicants need 10+ years' experience in packaging and corrugate production management with a detailed understanding of the entire process from design, printing and laminating to cutting, gluing and finishing. Ability to maintain relevant ISO and BS quality compliance is essential, as is the ability to continuously improve order to delivery times. Specialist knowledge of pharmaceutical packaging regulations an advantage.

Then you could say in your CV:

- ▶ 11 years managing all packaging processes with teams of up to 80 people.
- ▶ Successfully implementing ISO and BS quality compliance on three different sites.
- ▶ Devising innovative process solutions to reduce customer lead times by up to 20%.
- ▶ Introducing automated Braille equipment for pharmaceutical packaging in 2009.

Lower jargon levels reflect the advert better.

If this person were now leaving the printing industry for a job elsewhere, their points might be de-jargonized even further so that they could apply to any management role:

- ▶ 11 years' production management experience with teams of up to 80 people.
- ▶ Successfully introducing industry quality standards on three different sites.

- ▶ Devising innovative ways to reduce customer lead times by up to 20%.
- ▶ Staying ahead with clever equipment purchasing: e.g. winning new orders with AcuBraille (automated Braille embossing machine) for pharmaceutical customers.

Leaving out specific quality procedures or types of equipment makes it more generic, while specific details such as team size, number of sites and reduced lead times stay in as these are still important for proof. AcuBraille stays in as a good example, but is now explained.

Job titles

Loosely, the rules of jargon also apply to job titles. A supervisor in a coal mine may have a totally different type of role to a supervisor in a factory, or a supervisor in a telesales department. An account manager in one company may have a vastly different remit to an account manager in another.

So, like jargon, don't rely on job titles to bring instant understanding to your audience. This is another reason why it is so important to include your specific achievements and to demonstrate your level of skill in your Employment section.

TEN THINGS TO REMEMBER

1 *Jargon should be used to improve understanding.*

2 *You can't be sure who will end up reading your CV.*

3 *Only use jargon if there is no viable alternative.*

4 *Don't try to impress with jargon.*

5 *Take your lead from the amount of jargon in the job advert.*

6 *Jargon is less risky when applying for roles within the same industry.*

7 *Always explain jargon if you're applying to a new industry.*

8 *Job titles are like jargon: they don't mean the same in every company.*

9 *Try to balance being clear with being concise.*

10 *Test CV jargon on someone outside your industry to see if they understand it.*

Part four
Targeting it carefully

You've taken your factsheet, turned it into a chronological CV, and refined it so that it:

- includes the most powerful words possible
- remains honest
- smoothes problem areas
- uses jargon appropriately.

A well-written document is what you should now be looking at; but still a work in progress.

This is your 'generic CV'. This is the only kind of CV you can write without a specific industry, job or employer in mind. When you know you should have a CV, but don't really know how you'll end up using it, this is about as far as you can go.

This generic CV is your master document, which includes the basic material for every application you will send out. Only very rarely should you send this out as it stands.

Professionally written CVs

Generic CVs are often what you will receive from a professional CV writer. However brilliant they may be, there's not much more your writer can really provide if you haven't sent them details of the company and the job advert you are responding to, or if you don't even know (or haven't specified) the type of work you are looking for. Less brilliant writers may even create a generic CV no matter how much relevant detail you send them.

If you haven't asked your professional CV writer to tailor your CV to a specific vacancy, it is a good idea to request your generic CV as an editable electronic file – usually a Word document. Then you can easily adapt it yourself to target each opportunity. Don't feel tempted to save yourself time by sending out a generic CV without alteration: just changing the cover letter isn't usually enough.

Purchasing multiple hard copies of a professionally written CV therefore doesn't usually make sense, unless you are applying for an identical role within several different companies. Alternatively, if you really haven't a clue what job you want then you can send your generic CV out to several recruitment agencies to test the water. Agencies will often rewrite your generic CV to better target any opportunities they identify for you.

Target your CV every time

This crucial stage involves taking your generic CV and moulding it to suit the industry you want to work in, and then the company and role. Just like a sculptor, you will reshape some parts and lop others off altogether.

Whenever you see a position you want to apply for, or find a company you want to approach speculatively, always adapt your CV so it is properly targeted. Targeting doesn't have to take too long as you have done most of the groundwork already; but of course this is the stage you will repeat time and time again. Upfront it might take more time to get right, but getting your targeting spot on should mean you get more interviews and don't need to make as many applications in the long run.

Part four first looks at targeting by industry, then targeting by role.

IF YOU DON'T HAVE A COMPUTER

If you've written and refined everything by hand so far, your perseverance is to be admired – but now is the time to stop. Take your generic CV to the library, a friend, your children or parents, or even a typing service. Beg, borrow or pay, but try to get it typed into Microsoft Word and saved on a disk or memory stick.

Making changes by hand and retyping your CV time after time can be soul destroying. Targeting and presentation will seem to take forever – so you'll do anything to avoid it. And if you are paying someone to write up your CV, it'll cost a lot less to make changes from an existing generic file.

An electronic CV takes plenty of thought but just minutes to target, check and correct, which means you are much more likely to do it properly for each job you apply for.

10

Being specific (1) – targeting an industry

In this chapter you will:
- **highlight norms and expectations in different industries**
- **evaluate chronological, functional and hybrid CV types**
- **apply basic CV principles to your targeted CV.**

In general a finished, targeted CV should be one to two pages long and should contain some or all of the sections described in Part one, Preparing the details and Part two, Writing the basics. Creating a targeted CV from your generic CV, which may be much longer, means selecting the most relevant and powerful material to put in your one to two pages.

If you are unsure about what is required in a particular CV, bear in mind that a powerful, concise two-pager never offended anyone. However, it helps if your CV is appropriately constructed for the sector you are applying to and includes all the relevant details an employer would normally expect to see.

Understanding your sector and following some guidelines will help you to get it right.

Understand what the sector expects

Ask yourself what you will be doing, and what kinds of skills and knowledge are most likely to be valued. This question is obvious if you are a school leaver, graduate, or trying to change careers, but it does in fact apply to everyone. You can't tailor a CV effectively unless you know what is desirable.

Careers services, recruitment agencies and employers often provide useful summaries of different fields, online and offline. If you don't have easy access to a computer or other research facilities, try newspapers: reading a variety of job adverts for the industry you are interested in (not just those for roles you intend to apply for) will highlight common themes and desirable skills that you can demonstrate in your own CV.

Be genuinely enthusiastic about the field you are trying to get into

If railways are your passion, make sure it is clearly demonstrated in your CV when you apply for that job as a track maintenance technician or rail customer service adviser.

Genuine enthusiasm will help you stand out from a crowd of applicants who are simply desperate for any job as a technician or in customer service. Or just any job.

If it's your dream to work in Formula One, make sure your interest in and relevant experience with cars and motorsport is mentioned throughout your CV.

If you apply for a job in the Health and Beauty sector as office administrator for a large corporation, highlight your work experience at a salon between jobs, or your Beauty Therapy course at college. These will make your application appear more considered, and help it to be remembered.

Most companies want to attract and retain loyal employees. It's a far safer bet to recruit someone who'd love to work in their industry and who can show them why.

Follow industry expectations

There are many ways to divide up employment: sectors; segments; industries; fields.

Some people might consider retail banking, investment banking, financial planning and accounting to sit closely together under a single umbrella called Finance. But should financial sales also be included within Finance? Or Sales?

Unhelpfully, there are often no right or wrong answers. Every person or agency could justify dividing up the employment market in their own way.

However, some well-defined sectors may expect a CV that differs in length or detail, and would expect certain information that is not currently in your generic CV. The following list, while not exhaustive, is intended to give you a clearer guide to common expectations.

ACADEMIC/RESEARCH POSTS

For these types of positions include details of:

▶ academic posts held
▶ publications (single or joint, books, peer reviewed journals, edited articles, etc.)
▶ lectures, etc.

This can make your CV very lengthy if you have considerable academic qualifications and experience. However, you can still keep your CV brief and powerful using the techniques already described and then provide an appendix containing the above.

You could even cite web links for anyone interested in viewing publications or lecture transcripts in more detail.

TEACHING

For these types of positions include:

- ▶ degree subject as well, if PCGE
- ▶ relevant ongoing professional development/training
- ▶ awards and certificates (personal and school)
- ▶ all school experience/employment (even if applying for an executive position)
  - ▷ date
  - ▷ school (name, size and type)
  - ▷ year group/s taught
  - ▷ special projects
  - ▷ additional responsibilities
  - ▷ assessment methods
  - ▷ behaviour management strategies
  - ▷ special needs experience (personal and school)
- ▶ any upcoming experience
- ▶ interests relevant to teaching such as music, languages, sports, crafts, ICT, especially in a coaching capacity
- ▶ voluntary work, especially if related to teaching or summer camps.

Your introductory Profile or Summary could take the form of a 'Teaching statement': a short summary of your ideals, reasons for and approach to teaching, which gives some personal and professional insight into you.

MEDICAL

For these types of positions include:

- ▶ GMC registration number
- ▶ a career statement/objective that covers the specialist interests you are keen to develop, the research or teaching you wish to pursue, service development you want to become involved in, and any managerial ambitions. This is likely to be longer than the Objective in a typical CV, especially at consultant level

- ▶ 'relevant clinical experience'. Prioritize this in your Employment section but consider including 'Additional clinical experience' depending on the job you apply for.
- ▶ training courses straight after clinical experience (SHOs and Registrars)
- ▶ non-clinical experience (consultants). This means any teaching, management, research, publications, audits, presentations, etc.
- ▶ qualifications: you only need to include your medical degree and beyond, as A levels and GCSEs are largely irrelevant
- ▶ an awards/prizes section if you have enough to highlight: if you don't, make sure any are mentioned in your Employment section.

If you're coming from overseas to work in the UK:

- ▶ mention your eligibility to work in the UK (you don't have to provide evidence such as a visa or work permit at CV stage unless requested)
- ▶ it may help if you prioritize any UK medical experience
- ▶ demonstrate your English skills with International English Language Testing System (IELTS) and Professional & Linguistic Testing Board (PLAB) ratings.

Consultant CVs can run as high as 10 or 15 pages because of the amount of detail, but the basic rules still apply: your most important information should always be on page 1.

IT

Most IT work is project-based, so your CV will need to reflect this. You can do this in two ways:

1 For each employer, list the types of projects managed and benefits that resulted.
2 Group your projects by type and include a company-only employment history later.

Clearly summarize in separate Skills and Qualifications sections:

- ▶ technical/programming/networking skills you have (as proved in your project summary)
- ▶ relevant accreditation and other IT qualifications.

IT sector CVs are often longer and more functional in style (i.e. focusing on skills and projects managed, rather than a chronological employment history) but it's still very good practice to keep your CV length down to two pages – three at a push.

If you are targeting your CV carefully, you should be ruthless: some projects will not be as relevant as others and so can be cut. You can always reintroduce them at interview, if you feel they are an additional selling point.

DIPLOMATIC

For these types of positions include:

- ▶ a photograph (especially if applying overseas as photo CVs are more common)
- ▶ your nationality
- ▶ language skills: call them out in a separate section, be clear about your first language. If you are not sure how to classify your level of competence, try using the Europass classification system to determine your written and spoken ability (see Chapter 18 for details of further resources online)
- ▶ publications (books, articles and reports).

Some publication lists make a CV quite lengthy. Again, you can handle this by keeping in only the most relevant publications, by supplying an appendix, or citing web links for additional detail.

ENGINEERING

There is a belief within the industry that engineering CVs are longer and that this is acceptable. However, like any other industry, if you only include skills and experience that are most relevant to the job you are applying for, it doesn't automatically have to be significantly longer.

Any recruiter in any industry will thank you for being brief and to the point in your CV: they can always ask you more detailed questions at interview.

Like the IT industry, much engineering work is contract-based, so it may help to have a more functional style of CV. That means starting with a Key Skills summary (with proof examples of course), followed by a list of relevant projects completed – ideally grouped by type – and finally a brief list of dates and employers.

For these types of position include:

▶ whether you are a chartered or incorporated engineer
▶ a Skills summary next to, or as part of, your Summary or Profile
▶ nationality: some engineering jobs require complex security clearance for non-nationals to work in the UK so mention this, especially to employers that do MoD work
▶ language skills if you're applying to work for a multinational company
▶ driving licence, transport and relocation details – engineers rarely stay in one place, so it can help an employer or recruitment agency to know these details.

As for most jobs, experience is generally more relevant than education (and therefore comes earlier, i.e. on the front page) unless you are a recent graduate. Swap these sections around if needed so they sit in the right order for your circumstances.

If you are a recent graduate, in your Education section:

▶ mention all your degree modules
▶ include the subject of any projects/dissertations
▶ don't bother including details of A levels and GCSEs.

DEFENCE, ELECTRONICS, COMMUNICATIONS

For these types of position include:

- ▶ a list of product areas you've worked in: RF comms, satellite, broadcast, telecomms, data acquisition, etc.
- ▶ management techniques or project management methodologies, quality standards, Health and Safety, etc.
- ▶ familiarity with computer environments and languages and any programming ability, plus general software skills
- ▶ other relevant skills such as CAD, Test equipment used, etc.
- ▶ relevant additional courses and training you have undergone.

LEGAL

Legal firms place a much stronger focus on education than many other industries; even more so if you are a student or graduate applying for a vacation placement, work experience or a training contract.

Your research skills will also be of great interest, so don't let them down. Perhaps more than any other field, this is not an industry in which it is acceptable to send a generic CV with a 'standard' Summary and Objective. It must be tailored to each firm.

Education
Be sure to include:

- ▶ grades for all your educational qualifications from GCSE up to degree level
- ▶ names of institutions where you studied
- ▶ any awards or commendations
- ▶ details of modules studied

Research skills
Show off your research skills in a practical way. Demonstrate why you are interested in certain areas of law and why this firm above all others. Every firm has particular requirements and is only

interested in highly motivated applicants who have strong reasons to want to work for them. Present your research as a clear and logical but concise argument. This can be very effective when used in place of a more typical Summary and Objective at the start of your CV.

As well as the usual planning, research, analytical and reasoning skills, which should be clearly demonstrated in your skills examples, other skills may be relevant depending on the area of law, type of firm, and level of position you are applying for. Possessing commercial awareness, or client-facing experience, could be equally important – so ensure you tailor your CV carefully to bring out all these points.

Lengths of specialist CVs

Despite your best efforts, there will be some things you cannot fit onto two pages. These might cover:

- publications and lectures for a long-standing academic
- schools worked at for an experienced supply teacher
- complete project list for a long-qualified engineer
- all procedures performed by a consultant neurosurgeon
- an account of all a diplomat's research and policy recommendations.

This doesn't mean you can ignore relevance and brevity. It will still benefit you to select the most recent and meaningful examples.

If your aim when supplying this information is to show breadth or depth of experience, you can still refer to the quantity/scope of your work while listing only the highlights. Where full and specific details are requested, though, you will need to supply these. However, you could provide these in a supplement or appendix (as you might do with references) and therefore still leave your main CV powerfully concise.

If a lot of detail is truly unavoidable – or desirable – and you are sending this to a lot of employers, you could always try providing a brief summary on your CV and including a web link (if sending your CV electronically, a hyperlink) for the recruiter to view full details on a web page.

If you do this, ensure the link is correctly typed – and that it works – and that it only leads the person to relevant and correct information. Password-protect your web pages if you wish to prevent unauthorized viewing, especially if you are listing sensitive information about yourself or others (such as references). In case someone does not have web access, you may also wish to make a note on your CV that this information is also available in hard copy upon request.

Example: Academic publications

Sole author of 17 books on applied linguistics, psychology and recruitment, including:
Gott, I. T. 2010. *The Employers Handbook: Fifty ways to make job advertisements more effective*. London: HE Press.

Sole author of 93 peer-reviewed journal articles on applied linguistics, most recently:
Gott, I. T. 2010. Writing a stunning CV in twenty different languages. *Journal of Professional CV Writing*, 13(1), pp. 56–60.

Joint author of 286 peer-reviewed journal articles on the psychology of recruitment, most recently:
Gott, I. T. and Bing, O. 2010. Do you really expect me to believe that? Questions interviewers wish they didn't have to ask. *Journal of Advanced Interview Techniques*, 11(3), pp. 257–271.

For further publication details or copies of selected articles, please see my web page at www.gottit.co.uk, password: Blag1t. Hard copy available upon request.

Example: Teaching experience

Supply teaching at 74 UK schools in two-week to one-year stints. Adding value through extra-curricular activities, even on the shortest placement. Recent experience includes:

Oct 2009–May 2010, Years 6 & 7, St Trinian's Primary School, London

▶ Requested to undertake third maternity placement at the same school.
▶ Expanding popular street dance club established during second placement.
▶ Leading consultation on SEN facilities development and grant application.

Sept–Oct 2009, Year 6, Polporran Primary School, Cornwall

▶ Six-week position resulting in permanent job offer
▶ Raising £1,237 for school library by proposing and organizing Hallowe'en fundraising, gaining support and contributions from staff, parents and children.

Sept 2009, Year 7, North Camp Primary School, Derbyshire

▶ Two-week placement
▶ Wrote series of five-minute 'Lunchbox Stories' read aloud by staff on Friday lunchtimes. Different foods star each week, encouraging children to learn about foods and try

(Contd)

something new. Tradition continued. Negotiating book series with publisher.

For full details and references, visit my web page at www.born2teach.co.uk/supply, password: 5itdown.

Which type of CV to use

There are three main accepted CV formats:

▶ chronological (reverse chronological)
▶ functional
▶ hybrid (combination of chronological and functional).

CHRONOLOGICAL

The standard, most common CV type is the reverse chronological, which has everything in reverse date order. Up until this point, reverse chronological has been assumed because recruiters are more familiar with this than any other type. Provided a reverse chronological CV is well written, recruiters should be able to see easily if someone has the evidence and experience they seek.

Pros and cons
▶ All recruiters are very familiar with the format.
▶ It's quick to scan through.
▶ Your CV is easy to compare side by side with others.

But ...

▶ If your employment history is not great, it can be harder to do yourself justice.

Should you deem reverse chronological unsuitable for your circumstances or for a particular application, alternative formats do exist.

FUNCTIONAL

Given that content and layout should be relevant to the industry, company and job you are applying for, a functional CV might help display your talents more appropriately. This focuses on what you can **do**, based on the sum total of your experience.

Functional CVs don't list achievements and examples of skills in date order, by job or by employer. Instead they start by highlighting the most useful and transferable knowledge and skills that you offer, some career- or industry-specific and others more generic.

A functional CV format can work well if:

▶ your specialist experience is key
▶ you are changing career or industry
▶ you are applying for very senior positions
▶ you are a graduate or school leaver with little or no work experience
▶ you have had numerous different jobs, each for a short space of time
▶ your work is project-based in nature
▶ your work experience and/or knowledge spans more than one industry.

Depending on the field you apply for, a functional CV can work better than a chronological CV. If your skills and experience were gained through a long series of projects or assignments, the sum of what you can offer a future employer will carry more weight than a long list of past employers or projects.

Functional CVs are by no means common in many sectors, although they shouldn't be totally alien to any major recruiters.

Pros and cons

▶ Clear summary of the skills you offer: recruiters don't have to dig for details.
▶ Your functional competencies are obvious without reading your Employment section.
▶ Clusters lengthy or varied work and projects.
▶ Can help make your CV more concise.

But ...

▶ Some recruiters may be suspicious you are trying to conceal employment gaps.
▶ Recruiters unused to this format may find it more difficult to scan quickly.
▶ Can be harder to compare against reverse chronological CVs.

HYBRID

For the truly undecided, there is a third option called a hybrid CV: literally, a mix of chronological and functional. This can be a good option if you want the benefits of a functional CV and the spotlight on your skills, competencies and experience, but without quite going all the way.

Converting chronological CVs into other formats

Whichever format you prefer, your time spent preparing your generic CV in reverse chronological style has not been wasted. A well-written generic CV with clear examples is quite quick and easy to convert into a functional CV as part of the targeting process.

Let's say you are an accountant in a large firm. You began your career servicing small businesses and spent the last four years specializing in charities and non-profit organizations. You now want to apply your skills to a different industry to broaden your commercial understanding. Your specialist knowledge won't necessarily be an advantage to an employer in a different field.

However, your accounting ability, client-facing skills, team leadership, flexibility and willingness to continue to develop your knowledge will all be desirable. Your CV could therefore highlight your overall skills and abilities rather than focusing on exactly what you've done in each role.

So, simply rearrange your information so that before Employment is your Skills or Competencies section. The Employment section (if you have one) follows as a brief list of dates, job titles and employers.

If you have little work experience, you can draw examples for your Skills section from voluntary work, school, college, university or your personal life.

Military personnel pursuing a civilian career may also find this a more useful format, as it focuses less on the specifics of your military life and more on the transferable skills you have gained.

After the Skills section you may wish to include an Achievements section, following the same rules as above: you can draw your achievements from any time or any part of your life as long as they are relevant, but the more recent ones are most powerful.

EXAMPLE: REVERSE CHRONOLOGICAL CV

FIONA DE GENERA

Curric House, Ulum Road, Huntingdon, G1Z JO8
Tel: 01234 567 890
Email: fidegenera@gmail.com

Profile

A chartered accountant and skilled finance director, I wish to capitalize on my technical knowledge and practical experience of financial accounting and taxation, in the role of ICAEW exam
(Contd)

marker covering these modules: my starting point for a career in accountancy training.

Achievements

▶ Recognized in 2008 Who's Who of Britain's Business Elite as owner of one of Britain's most successful businesses.

Career History

2007–present   Consultant, Wingover Logistics, Luton

Wingover is a specialist international courier with an average annual turnover of £15m.

▶ Advising on annual business strategy and assessing new investment opportunities to drive growth by 28 per cent year on year while maintaining profitability.
▶ Reviewing monthly management accounts and year end financial statements.
▶ Assisting with preparation of successful business tenders for international clients.

2005–2007   Finance Director, Wingover Logistics

▶ Responsible for devising and implementing financial strategy as a member of the Board.
▶ Working closely with the CEO and MD to shape overall business strategy and direction.
▶ Overseeing all financial operations and day-to-day accountancy, including preparing year end financial statements and draft tax computations.

2001–2005   Manager Roles, Silva & Gold Chartered Accountants, Worksop

Youngest ever manager after qualification for this national firm with £150m annual fee income.

2003–2005   **Audit Department Manager**

▶ Promoted to be part of the eight-strong audit management team, with a staff of 30.
▶ Specializing in charity accounts and larger private companies.
▶ Overseeing accounts production and auditing using an analytical review approach.

2001–2003   **Small Business Unit Manager**

▶ Overseeing teams of 1–10 preparing accounts for small businesses, sole traders and partnerships.
▶ Co-ordinating and supervising a pool of 25 staff as part of a four-strong management team.
▶ Assistant training manager for students.

1998–2001   **Audit Junior/Senior, Silva & Gold Chartered Accountants**

Professional Memberships

▶ Member of the Association of Chartered Accountants (2001)

Education

2001   Association of Chartered Accountants
1998   BA (Hons) 2:1 in Tourism and Leisure, University of Truro
1994   3 A Levels
1992   10 GCSEs

IT Skills

▶ Sage Line 50 and Viztopia accounting software
▶ Microsoft Office Suite

(Contd)

- ▶ Qualified First Aider (2006)
- ▶ Full clean driving licence

To convert this to a functional CV is relatively straightforward:

EXAMPLE: FUNCTIONAL CV

FIONA DE GENERA

Curric House, Ulum Road, Huntingdon, G1Z JO8
Tel: 01234 567 890
Email: fidegenera@gmail.com

Objective

A chartered accountant and successful finance director, I wish to capitalize on my technical knowledge of financial accounting and taxation in the role of ICAEW exam marker covering these modules. My intent is to pursue a career in accountancy training.

Key Skills and Competencies

Technical Knowledge

- ▶ Experience preparing, co-ordinating and auditing financial accounts using an analytical approach, for small, medium and large business clients and charities while at Silva & Gold.
- ▶ Overseeing management accounts, resolving complex financial planning and taxation issues, analysing and making recommendations on new investments for the highly successful Wingover Logistics.

General Management

- ▶ Planning, allocating and managing resources as the Finance Director for Wingover Logistics: collaborating on four successful tenders, two for the highly competitive defence industry.

- Measuring and monitoring audit team activities to improve processes at Silva & Gold, saving 23 man hours per week across a team of 30 staff.

Leadership

- Successful organizational and strategic leadership as Finance Director of Wingover Logistics.
- Quickly promoted to lead the Small Business team at Silva & Gold, personally responsible for student training and staff development, before becoming Audit Manager within two years.

Achievements

- Recognized in 2008 Who's Who of Britain's Business Elite as owner of one of Britain's most successful businesses.
- Youngest ever manager at Silva & Gold upon qualification.

Professional Memberships

- Member of the Association of Chartered Accountants (2001)

IT Skills

- Sage Line 50 and Viztopia accounting software
- Microsoft Office Suite

Career Summary

2005–present   **Wingover Logistics, Heathrow**

Specialist international courier company: average annual turnover £15m.

2007–present   **Consultant**
2005–2007   **Finance Director**

(Contd)

National mid-tier independent accountancy firm: annual fee income £150m.

2003–2005	**Audit Department Manager**
2001–2003	**Small Business Unit Manager**
1998–2001	**Audit Junior/Senior**

Education

2001	Association of Chartered Accountants
1998	BA (Hons) 2:1 in Tourism and Leisure, University of Truro

Further Details

▶ Qualified First Aider (2006)
▶ Full clean driving licence

Employment gaps

Don't see functional or hybrid CVs as a cure-all for gaps in your employment – they aren't. You still need to list your previous employment and dates worked. However, a functional or hybrid CV can help by drawing the eye to your skills and abilities first and foremost, helping you to make that all-important good impression before any gaps become apparent.

A final word on format

Whichever CV format you choose, the same generic chronological CV is your starting point. The same rules for writing, refining and targeting apply – and format is determined when you start to target particular industries, companies and jobs.

A good chronological CV should highlight your skills and competencies in the Summary at the beginning anyway, so in some ways it's a matter of degrees when it comes to how chronological or functional a CV type you feel happy using.

If you are really unsure, try creating more than one final CV from your generic CV and ask friends or colleagues for their views. A specialist recruitment agent can also be a great source of advice if you have specific questions about what to include at this stage, although every employer and recruiter may have certain preferences that are personal rather than industry oriented. When talking to recruitment agencies, do ensure your CV is as refined and targeted as possible before you contact them, in case they ask to see it.

TEN THINGS TO REMEMBER

1 *If it's new to you, research the sector you want to be working in.*

2 *If certain skills are highly prized, ensure they feature strongly in your CV.*

3 *Explain why you want to work in this sector: provide evidence.*

4 *Follow sector guidelines and include essential details.*

5 *Remain focused on creating a short and relevant CV.*

6 *Try to provide appendices or web links with further details, especially if lengthy.*

7 *Your generic CV should be a 'standard' reverse chronological type.*

8 *Targeted CVs can be chronological, functional or hybrid: converting is simple.*

9 *Each CV type has potential pros and cons.*

10 *If unsure what to include in your CV or the best type to use, ask for feedback.*

11

Being specific (2) – targeting a job and employer

In this chapter you will:
- *identify which skills and competencies are important for the role you want*
- *learn how to win over people and automated scanners*
- *understand the role of research in effective targeting*

The role

Once you've got a handle on the industry or sector you're hoping to work in, and have structured your CV accordingly, you must tailor it to the specific role that you are after.

To do this successfully, you first need to know which skills and competencies are essential to be able to do this job well (at least in the employer's eyes, which may or may not always reflect reality), and which other skills may also be beneficial. This can be straightforward or may need some additional research on your part.

Skills and competencies

RESPONDING TO A JOB ADVERT

This makes it easy: the job advert lays out a concise list of the key competencies and experience that a company is looking for in an ideal applicant. The priorities – whether a particular skill is essential or just nice to have – are usually made clear.

It cannot be stressed enough how crucial it is to read a job advert carefully. Writing down two lists as you read through it, one for the requirements considered essential, the other for the nice-to-haves, can help you focus on what's important.

This is purely the company's wish list: don't be put off if you don't meet every single requirement 100 per cent, as many other candidates probably won't be able to either. However, realistically you should meet at least 75 per cent of the essential requirements and have other skills you can 'sell' in order to be considered seriously. If you meet less than 75 per cent of the criteria, your chances of getting an interview – particularly in a job-scarce climate – could be slight. It's up to you whether you spend the time and money applying anyway, or focus on those job specifications that you meet more closely.

When assessing how well you meet the requirements of a job and what else you could offer, try comparing similar job adverts from other companies: ones for distant locations or other industries. There will be much overlap, but every now and again you may see a skill mentioned that you hadn't thought of; one you could sell as a benefit to this employer.

Examples of adverts for sales roles on one date

Weighing solutions: Formal sales training, AM experience, a technical background.
Self-organization, attention to detail, target-driven, tenacious, resilient.
Computer literate. Full UK driving licence.

Medical equipment: Proven sales track record, confident communicator and presenter.
Commercially astute, comfortable discussing finance and capex budgets at director level.
A will to win, real drive, ambition, tenacious, organized, able to prioritize. Team player also able to work autonomously, personal charisma, a real 'people person'.

Facilities Management: Proven sales track record in services, solutions and FM contracts. Excellent communicator who can present, negotiate and close sales at board level. Commercially astute, team player, motivator, capable, enthusiastic, organized.
A will to win, engaging personality, relationship builder, computer literate, able to prioritize.

PAT Testing & Maintenance: Proven track record in Fire, Security or related sales. Professional presentation, communication and networking skills.
Ambitious, confident, organized. Able to travel: role covers the whole of the UK.

Pest & Vermin Control: Proven track record in sales to SMEs and large companies.
Strong communicator and presenter, comfortable negotiating and closing sales at all levels.
Team player, confident personality, punctual, honest, motivated and able to listen. Computer literate, organized, able to prioritize and deliver results.

Recruitment: Great communication skills to work with people at all levels.
Determined, self-motivated, resilient, tenacious.
Ambitious, energetic, goal orientated, highly driven to exceed targets.

Based on these examples, there are several essential skills or attributes common to most sales roles:

- ▶ proven sales success
- ▶ commercial awareness
- ▶ communication skills
- ▶ presentation skills
- ▶ negotiation skills
- ▶ interpersonal skills: a team player, personal charisma, a relationship builder
- ▶ drive/ambition, motivated/determined, resilient, will to win/ goal orientated, tenacious.

Further desirable criteria might include:

- ▶ experience selling in a particular field or product type
- ▶ computer literacy, organization skills, ability to prioritize
- ▶ full UK driving licence, ability to travel
- ▶ energetic, enthusiastic, punctual, honest, good listener.

The 'essential' list in the job advert you are responding to is the one you should focus on meeting with your targeted CV, and it is very likely to reflect the first list.

If you can prove you have attributes from the second list, which would also be useful for a salesperson and could benefit your employer, then these can be great additional selling points – particularly if you are lacking one of the 'essential' elements.

Automated scanning software

When you write down the list of required skills, use exactly the same language as the advert. Then reflect this in your CV.

Each recruiter will be looking for evidence of skills in the CVs and covering letters they receive, and those processing a lot of applications may use automated scanning software to pick up these key words. For your CV to be as effective as possible, you need to achieve as many matches as you can. This doesn't mean simply repeating everything word for word. Recruiters want to see how well you meet the spec, not just that you can copy out their advert. Use your own phrasing, but include their key words.

Insight

Automated scanning software only looks for key words and phrases, it isn't usually sophisticated enough to understand the context in which you use them. So, even if you don't meet a particular requirement, find a way to mention it anyway; but make sure you 'sell' an alternative skill as your CV will probably be read by a human next.

Examples

Job advert: Minimum two years' sales experience, ideally in the pharmaceutical sector.

You have two years' sales experience but in fmcg (fast moving consumer goods), not pharmaceuticals. You could say in your CV profile or covering letter: 'Nearly *two years' sales experience* in fmcg, highly transferable to the *pharmaceutical sector*.'

These two key words or phrases would get picked up by the scanning software as 'hits'. This improves your chances of getting to the next stage versus someone who doesn't mention it at all. The scanner won't recognize that you are admitting you don't meet this requirement but selling yourself in other ways. This gives you a realistic shot of staying in the 'yes' pile until the next stage when real people will read your CV.

(Contd)

Job advert: Five years' marketing experience.

You only have two years' marketing experience, but your background is in sales. Your CV profile or covering letter could say: *'Five years' experience in marketing* and sales, giving me an invaluable perspective that ensures marketing activities are truly beneficial to the sales team.'

The first half will be picked up as a key word or phrase 'hit', while the second half suggests to the human reader that your combined sales experience is even better than marketing experience alone.

Job advert: Must be an experienced public speaker.

Your covering letter could say: 'While not an *experienced public speaker* per se, I regularly conduct training sessions for groups of 30 or more people, and believe my outstanding presentation skills are highly transferable to the role in question.'
Keyword hit.
You could put something similar (but not identical) into your CV profile:
'Much in demand as a trainer of large groups, with excellent communication and presentation skills comparable to those of an *experienced public speaker.'*
Keyword hit again, whilst emphasizing your core skills.

APPLYING SPECULATIVELY

Of course in this case there will be no current job advert, but that doesn't need to put a damper on things. The company you are targeting may have recruited into the role you'd like in the past, and with a bit of digging you can sometimes find old job adverts and descriptions online.

Other companies, whether in the same or different industry, may be recruiting into similar positions too. Check their job adverts as well, to establish the common competencies desired for all such roles. You may also find mention of other skills you might 'sell'.

If you know someone (a colleague, friend, family member or acquaintance) who does a similar type of role, give them a call. Most people are more than happy to help when asked for advice, and they may be able to give you a better insight into the most desirable skills. As an added benefit, they may even know about unadvertised vacancies within their own organization that you could speculatively apply for.

Some companies may keep your details on file for a long time, adding your CV to the application pile when a vacancy arises. Bear in mind the same guidelines on automated scanning software: ensure you use the most common key words and phrases in your speculative CV too.

So, how do you tailor your CV based on the details you've discovered about the role?

Reverse chronological CVs

PROFILE

Include as many keywords and phrases from the job advert as you can, while making them specific and relevant to you. Promote transferable skills in lieu of experience if you are lacking experience, and give your rationale.

EMPLOYMENT HISTORY

Focus first on the demonstration of skill examples that show the essential skills required. Then add in the nice-to-have skills, before selling other benefits you can offer. Where possible draw your examples from similar roles or employment in a related industry that could benefit the position you are applying for.

Don't give example after example from your two years spent quietly in a back office doing purchase ledger entries on your own if you're applying for a consumer sales job, while ignoring that fortnight-long summer holiday job you had working commission-only in a high street bank call centre ...

FURTHER SKILLS

Again, relevance is the buzz word. You might want to show off all your skills, but not all of them are necessarily going to help you do *this* job better.

Generally speaking, being fluent in Japanese (whilst impressive) won't benefit a SAP project manager who is based in the UK, unless you manage international projects. Likewise, programming in C++ doesn't really increase your suitability for insurance sales, and a forklift or HGV licence matters little if you are after an office job.

A few skills may be useful to any role: a First Aid At Work or Health and Safety qualification, or a clean driving licence may well hold more universal appeal, although these often won't be on the essential skills list.

INTERESTS

Many people think this is just a section to get employers to remember them, or for sparking off an interview warm-up. In some cases it is. But it's a safer bet to use it in the same way as the rest of your CV – for maximum selling impact.

If one of your interests helps to demonstrate the skills required for the job, especially skills not shown at work, don't be afraid to describe the interest in a little more detail. Good team captains show leadership; club treasurers show financial acumen; part-time referees show judgement, decisiveness and in some cases conflict resolution; amateur dramatics suggests confidence and clear speaking in front of a large audience; a junior football coach might possess strong training and/or mentoring skills.

Functional CVs

SKILLS/COMPETENCIES

Your Skills or Competencies section should reflect in priority order the essential and nice-to-have skills as mentioned in the job advert, with supporting evidence. Add on any additional skills you could argue would be beneficial to the role, but leave out any that you really don't need to show.

All CVs

ACHIEVEMENTS

If you include one, this section should be focused on achievements relevant to the job advert, although you can be a little creative.

Grade 8 piano, whilst an impressive achievement, is completely irrelevant for a maintenance engineer – so just leave it out. Undertaking a World Challenge community project overseas with 15 of your peers might not instantly shout 'salesperson', but when you highlight the teamwork, communication skills and motivation that its successful completion required, then you're directly answering the advert.

Generally speaking, you want to have two or more bullet points before you create a separate achievements section, unless the achievement is particularly powerful, current and relevant to the role, in which case you could highlight just one.

If you have only one or two rather weak or old achievements to talk about and don't feel comfortable shouting about them in a separate section, but they are relevant to the job, include them in your Employment History or Interests, as appropriate.

If you are not sure whether an achievement is strong or weak, ask a friend. Are they impressed by it in the context of the job you want?

LENGTH

A targeted CV is likely to be shorter than the generic version. Basic maths suggests that if you meet 75 per cent of the job advert requirements, you should include a *maximum* of 75 per cent of the examples from your employment history. Given that not all examples will be relevant and, of those that are, you only want the best and most recent, your targeted Employment section should be significantly shorter than the one on your generic CV.

RELEVANCE

Critical point: a fuller CV does not make you look any more proficient or experienced in the reader's eyes. All it says is that you waffle a lot or have not read the advert properly. Either way it's too much effort to dig through it for the information they want.

No role exists in a vacuum. While there will be many similarities between the same role in different companies, a significant part of your CV tailoring should be determined by the employer.

The employer

Research market, company and audience background as much as possible. This won't just stand you in good stead for CV writing but will make it much easier when you come to interview as well. Research can be very helpful for a number of reasons, but if you lack experience then some solid research can help you appear much more confident and knowledgeable, whilst ensuring you relate what experience you do have to the role.

MARKET

In some cases, especially larger corporations, you may not know which company is actually doing the hiring. This is because you are asked to send your CV to a recruitment agency. Obviously you won't be expected to know anything about the employer at first, but it can certainly help if you know a bit about the marketplace.

Marketing strategy (and the end consumers it is aimed at) is likely to be quite different at an fmcg ('fast moving consumer goods') company compared to a luxury yacht company, a manufacturer of interactive school learning resources or an automotive lubricant developer. Someone applying for a marketing position at the fmcg company would probably benefit from market research experience at a snack foods manufacturer. A luxury yacht salesman would benefit from sales experience at a vintage sports car dealership. The school resources product range would benefit from someone who has insight from working part-time as a teaching assistant. Experience in a technical or automotive environment would add the most value to the automotive lubricant company.

Example

You are currently working in vintage sports car sales and fancy a job in luxury yacht sales, but have no yacht sales experience. If you don't know the company name, your research might look like this:

▶ Use the internet to learn whether the market for yachts is growing or shrinking.
▶ Check out the main players: who they are and which ones are performing well – or poorly.
▶ Find out as much as you can about luxury yachts, specs and owners in general.

(Contd)

- What sort of costs are you looking at: are the yachts in the lower and middle price ranges similar in cost to the cars you currently sell?
- Look into consumer lifestyles to see if yacht owners tend to also own vintage cars.

You could have some strong selling points in the experience you already have. You might argue that you understand the consumer, and have a proven track record in high value sales. Obviously if you are an avid sailor yourself, that will certainly help.

In this case you can use all this research to tailor your:

- Profile: sell your 'relevant' sales experience and consumer understanding.
- Objective: why you want to sell yachts and feel you are suited to it.
- Experience: highlight examples of success in selling high end luxury goods.
- Interests: (all sailing and water-focused activities).

COMPANY

If you do know the name of the company that is recruiting (or you ring the recruitment consultant and they are happy to tell you), it helps. Internet research can also give you insight into almost anything, including the:

- company culture
- kind of people they attract
- products they make
- main competitors for their business
- current and past performance.

This can be useful in the same way as your marketplace research, but with the added benefit of being much more specific.

Your reason for applying

If you don't already have a sound reason for wanting to work for a particular employer, then use your research to develop a rationale. It might seem a little strange to find a company first and then find a reason why you want to work for them, but it really is important. Otherwise you can imagine how the conversation might go:

> **Employer:** 'So, how do I know that you really want to work for us?'
> **Applicant:** 'Well, I applied for a job here didn't I?'
> **Employer:** 'Hmm … I mean why us, and not one of our competitors?'
> **Applicant:** 'No one else is advertising at the moment.'
> **Employer:** 'Thank you for your honesty. Next!'

When doing research, look out for any details that could help you explain not just 'why I'm looking for this kind of role' but 'why I really want this role in *your* company'. Having a positive story about why you'd love to work for a particular employer – it doesn't have to be long and involved – will shine through on your CV, and at interview.

Example

Pinocchio is a small, rapidly growing manufacturer of innovative wooden toys made from sustainable timber. Companies House accounts show it has been established for five years and has turned a good annual profit for the last three years. You own several of the company's toys as you prefer environmentally sound products, and you also see them advertised. Your research suggests that market share of wooden toys is growing because of their environmental benefits and long-lasting value.

(Contd)

Your Objective could read:

Good

Looking to broaden my experience by applying my selling skills to another industry, building long-term relationships while promoting new and interesting products.

Better

Looking to broaden my consumer sales experience by building business-to-business relationships to drive sales of innovative product ranges such as Pinocchio's.

Best

Looking to broaden my proven sales ability in a business-to-business context. Hoping to use my strong rapport and negotiation skills to support rapid growth, ideally for an innovative company like Pinocchio: its fantastic range of wooden toys particularly appeals to my passion for environmentally friendly products.

While the last objective is a little longer than the first, it mentions specific skills, your understanding of what the company does, and why this would be your dream job.

If Pinocchio was your company, would you want to interview the person with the standard spiel, or the person who really seems to like your products?

This kind of targeting is a fantastic way to instantly set yourself apart from other applicants. Ensure you also highlight the reasons why you want to work for this employer in the covering letter or email you send with your CV.

Protect yourself

Insight

Employers are not the only people who should be cautious: look out for yourself when researching companies at any time, but particularly when the economy is turbulent. You don't want to land that new job or change your career only to find your new position disappears within weeks because the company is in financial trouble.

Even the smallest companies usually have some kind of a website that will afford you some background information, although the smaller the company the sketchier it can be. Companies House allows you to look up the accounts of any UK-registered limited company, whatever their size, to see how they are performing financially.

All research is useful

None of this role, company or marketplace research should ever be considered a waste of time, even if you don't get the first interview you go for. Everything you find out about each company will contribute to your overall market understanding and you can refer back to it as you go through interviews or submit further applications.

TEN THINGS TO REMEMBER

1 *Analyse job adverts to identify skills/competencies you should focus on.*

2 *Be realistic about whether you meet enough core requirements.*

3 *Check similar adverts to see which additional skills are a bonus.*

4 *Reflect key words from adverts in your CV.*

5 *Fool scanners by mentioning key skills without actually claiming to have them.*

6 *Always sell alternative skills or experience when fooling the scanner.*

7 *If you can't find out about the company, research the marketplace instead.*

8 *A targeted CV should be shorter than your generic CV.*

9 *Protect yourself by checking company performance before you apply.*

10 *No research is wasted: each bit will help you build confidence.*

Part five

Presenting it perfectly

Now it's time to talk about presentation. Many people start with this aspect or focus on it more than any other but ultimately, however good a CV looks, it must stand up to scrutiny when read. For this reason content, style and relevance are the first areas this book tackles. Presentation is the final touch once the other aspects have been finalized.

Spending too much time on presentation can be a sign that you lack confidence in content, particularly if you are the kind of person who plays around with endless templates and layouts before you even start writing.

However, it must be admitted that great content and style can be severely damaged by poor presentation. Visual science and psychology back this up. Inappropriate presentation can make it harder for readers to pick out key points, and might even stop them from wanting to try. Studies have even suggested that poor presentation puts people in an irritable mood, while good presentation makes them happier. Happy is good, when someone is reading about you and deciding whether or not to invite you to interview.

Presentation is made up of three aspects:

- **layout** (fonts, colours, balance of text and space, line spacing, bullets, etc.)
- **quality control** (i.e. proofreading: spelling, grammar, punctuation and consistency)
- **physical format** (printed vs. digital; paper quality and colour; file format).

Layout and quality control are dealt with in Chapter 12, while physical format is covered in Chapter 13.

Your CV has to be instantly appealing and easily readable by any person (or machine) who picks it up. This means anyone: of any age or level of knowledge, with any level of experience, with little or no time to spare ... or with limited or restricted reading ability. They might be brilliant at their job but not keen on reading or perhaps dyslexic. It's likely that if you apply to just five companies and your CV is read by four people in each company, one of them will be dyslexic. Around one in 20 people in the UK is estimated to be dyslexic to some degree, whether they are aware of it or not. As a result, many of the tips on presentation aim to make your text as readable as possible to someone who has dyslexia. Taking into account the needs of dyslexics loses you nothing: you'll simply be making your CV easier for everyone to read.

12

···

Layout – how should a finished CV look?

In this chapter you will:
- *make your CV legible, scannable and readable*
- *ensure your CV is error-free*

You have already put a lot of work into content and style. Now it's time to perfect the layout to make sure your CV is read, understood and remembered.

The basic elements of good layout are drawn from years of scientific study into how people look at, read and process information. There are three things you must get right. A CV needs to be:

▶ legible
▶ scannable
▶ readable.

Getting these right means a CV that begs to be picked up and that won't be forgotten.

Making your CV legible

This simply means that someone can clearly make out the letters and words in your CV. It's amazing how often people get carried away making a page look 'pretty', or trying to fit too much onto two pages. Looking inviting is important, but don't forget the purpose of your CV is to be read and understood.

Here are some basic legibility guidelines:

▶ **Don't** spend hours picking out complex fonts that look nice – these can be hard to read.

Profile

A freelance marketing consultant with a highly creative yet proven commercial approach. Winner of ten industry awards for planning and executing successful branding and launch campaigns, including Yobabes organic yoghurt, Exobet online betting services and Pinx fashion accessories.

▶ **Do** use simple, clear fonts: for printed CVs, popular serif or sans serif fonts are both fine. It's okay to mix two fonts like newspapers do, for example, sans serif for headlines, serif for body text:

Profile

A freelance marketing consultant with a highly creative yet proven commercial approach. Winner of industry awards for planning and executing successful branding and launch campaigns, such as 2009's Yobabes organic yoghurt drink, Exobet online betting services and Pinx fashion accessories.

For online CVs, sans serif fonts are better as they are more legible on screen. If you are likely to send your CV on both paper and email, stay with sans serif.

Changing fonts back and forth can alter your page layout so once you find a font or a combination of fonts that you like, it's best to stick to it.

The most popular fonts are popular for a reason: now is not the time to be different. Times New Roman is the classic serif font, and is still the most common in printed material. Arial, Verdana and Tahoma are all common sans serif fonts.

Try to avoid fonts like Courier New as they can look rather primitive on a CV.

SIZE

▶ **Don't** think tiny text will help you to cram in more words – they end up too small to read easily.

▶ **Don't** use text smaller than 10 point as it is too hard for most people to read easily. This example is 9 point:

Profile

A desktop publishing expert with a graphic design background and a real flair for eye-catching imagery, demonstrated while designing press campaigns for products such as Dymond Bling at advertising agency GGH. Strong commercial awareness gained from three years in the wholesale sector, producing weekly price offer flyers to tight deadlines. A well-respected team player who makes a measurable contribution with good humour, both inside and outside work: currently treasurer of the sports and social club.

▶ **Do** use a big enough text size. 11–12 point is normal for body text, 14–16 point for headings.

Profile

A desktop publishing expert with a graphic design background and a real flair for eye-catching imagery, demonstrated while designing press campaigns for products such as Dymond Bling at advertising agency GGH. Strong commercial awareness gained from three years in the wholesale sector, producing weekly price offer flyers to tight deadlines. A well-respected team player who makes a measurable contribution

(Contd)

with good humour, both inside and outside work: currently
treasurer of the sports and social club.

LINE SPACING

▶ **Don't** squash lines close together to fit in more text – closely-
  spaced lines are harder to follow.

Profile

Newly-qualified veterinary nurse with six months' work
experience in a busy, city-based small animal practice. I
have a gift for handling animals calmly and safely, but my
real skill is in using interpersonal skills to set clients at ease –
especially when managing sensitive situations such as the
loss of a pet. Many clients already ask for me by name.

▶ **Do** always leave single line spacing as your default and don't
  be tempted to decrease it, however much you are struggling to
  fit something in. If the text won't fit two pages, delete the least
  relevant point/s on your CV.

Profile

Newly-qualified veterinary nurse with six months' work experience in a
busy, city-based small animal practice. I have a gift for handling animals
calmly and safely, but my real skill is in using interpersonal skills to set
clients at ease – especially when managing sensitive situations such as
the loss of a pet. Many clients already ask for me by name.

FONT EFFECTS

▶ **Don't** overuse font effects, and particularly try to avoid *italics*
  and CAPITALS. Both are harder to read than standard text.

Profile

*SKILLED ACOUSTIC ENGINEER WITH 17 YEARS'
EXPERIENCE IN THE MUSIC INDUSTRY, THE PAST*

TEN AS SHINY HOUSE STUDIO'S RESIDENT ENGINEER – WORKING WITH BANDS NEW AND OLD LIKE DUBDUB, NBT AND THE LIGHTNING TWINS. TECHNICALLY OUTSTANDING, I ALSO POSSESS STRONG COMMUNICATION AND INTERPERSONAL SKILLS WHICH ENABLE ME TO GET THE BEST RESULT FROM ANY SINGER.

▶ **Do** use plain font as standard. Bold is acceptable for highlighting headings or specific points, but use it sparingly.

Profile

Skilled acoustic engineer with 17 years' experience in the music industry, the past ten as Shiny House Studio's resident engineer – working with bands new and old, such as DubDub, NBT and The Lightning Twins. Technically outstanding, I also possess strong communication and interpersonal skills which enable me to get the best result from any singer.

Text alignment

▶ **Don't** justify the text even if it looks 'tidier'. Justifying text makes the spacing between words uneven, and this makes it harder to read.

Profile

Logistics operative with two years' experience at an international freight forwarding company learning all aspects of legislation, load planning, routing and customs documentation. Promoted within a year for making exceptional cost savings during the recent fuel crisis. Success driven by interpersonal skills, which enabled me to gain respect and cooperation from experienced drivers, who have come to appreciate my ability, sense of humour and assertiveness.

▶ **Do** always align text on the left-hand side, leaving the right side of the text 'ragged'.

Profile

Logistics operative with two years' experience at an international freight forwarding company learning all aspects of legislation, load planning, routing and customs documentation. Promoted within a year for making exceptional cost savings during the recent fuel crisis. Success driven by interpersonal skills, which enabled me to gain respect and cooperation from experienced drivers, who have come to appreciate my ability, sense of humour and assertiveness.

The reasoning behind the rules

FONT CHOICE

For years people have argued over whether sans serif fonts are easier to read than serif fonts. (Sans serif fonts, like Arial, Verdana or Tahoma, use letters without the little 'finishing strokes' that serif fonts like Times New Roman or Bookman Old Style have.)

This text is Times New Roman and has serifs.

This text is Verdana and has no serifs (sans serif).

There is a general belief that sans serif fonts are easier to read. For children, sans serif fonts have been shown to help with letter recognition, although it's not clear whether this also holds true for adults.

It may be as simple as personal preference, but it is interesting that most books and novels still use serif fonts. Perhaps it is because these are most widely accepted, but the serifs are also believed to help lead the eyes from one letter to the next. This makes it easier to follow each line when reading a long piece of text. But a CV is no novel – in fact the opposite, it is a very short document. Therefore one can assume small chunks of text can easily be followed without serifs to lead the eye.

In short, both sans serif and serif fonts are fine for a printed CV, provided the text is legible. For onscreen CVs, things are a little different: sans serif fonts are the norm. Not only are sans serif fonts easier to read on screen, they also reproduce more consistently on screen, unlike some serif fonts.

SIZE, SPACING AND EFFECTS

This is fairly self-evident: letters and words that are too small, closely bunched or distorted in some way will take longer to recognize and therefore understand.

ALIGNMENT

Leaving the right-hand side of text ragged is thought to simplify reading by making it easier to follow from the end of one line to the start of the next line.

Making your CV scannable (not the same as automated scanning!)

Once you have legible text, arranging it in a common sense, clear way is what makes it scannable: that is, easy for a person to scan through and quickly find what they want.

There are lots of things that make a CV more scannable:

- ▶ short text
- ▶ logical order
- ▶ clear headings and subheadings

- small chunks of information
- highlighted points: bullets, shading, dividing lines, boxed text
- use of white space.

Bear in mind that the more complex the formatting – things like shading, lines and boxes – the longer it will take you to edit and the more likely it is to end up looking different on someone else's screen. There is nothing wrong with a straightforward CV template in which the text is broken up with clear headings, bullet points and white space.

There are plenty of templates available online from numerous sources (see Chapter 18 for more details) which you can experiment with if desired.

Some general guidelines:

Don'ts
Don't add extra, unnecessary detail.

- Anything that wasn't already included will make your CV harder to scan through.

Don't change the order of your CV just to 'stand out from the crowd'.

- If you don't give readers what they expect, they will struggle to find details quickly.

Don't make headings too small or remove subheadings to save space.

- Headings are what signpost the reader to the important points in your CV.

Don't add extra text to make something look more important than it is.

- Longer text can hide key points. If it is important, just make it easy to find.

Don't run sentences into each other to save space.

- Bulleted lists will help individual points stand out best – shading can also help.

Don't fill every blank space on the page.

- Empty space is rarely a waste: documents with no blank spaces are daunting to read.

Dos
Do keep text short.

- Be disciplined. If it wasn't in when you refined your CV, it doesn't need to be added now.
- If you have missed out something really important, then decide which point it will replace.

Do make headings and subheadings clear.

- Again, stick to standard section headings so people know roughly what to expect in each.
- Headings must be big enough to stand out when you quickly run your eyes down the page.

Do have small chunks of information.

- People process small chunks of information best: break up text into chunks and space out.
- Each chunk should cover a separate point or subject.
- Headings should ideally have no more than five to seven bullet points under them.

Do highlight key points.

- Draw the reader's eye with easy bulleted lists, the top point being most important.
- You can also use subtle shading to highlight key sections, but do it carefully.

Always
Always have plenty of white space.

- ▶ White space makes a CV easier to read so it is more likely to be glanced at. Spaces outline each distinct section, leading the eye from one section to the next. Balancing text and space symmetrically can make a CV seem more attractive to read.

Always have a logical order.

- ▶ Stick to a familiar or 'expected' CV order, so readers know where to look for things. If you don't keep the order logical, the result can be a bit like going to your local supermarket to find they've changed the layout without warning. Suddenly all the products you usually pick up in minutes aren't where you expected them to be: your shop takes twice as long as usual and you feel irritated.
- ▶ Check all dates are in consistent chronological (usually reverse chronological) order.
- ▶ Make sure headings relate to the text that comes just below them – this is easy to overlook, especially if you cut and paste a lot.

Readability

The final aim of your CV is to be readable – easy to read. Some of these points have already been covered while creating your generic CV, but it's worth checking again that your finished CV is still very readable.

What makes a CV readable (in addition to legibility and scannability, of course) is a mixture of word length and sentence length.

WORD LENGTH

Longer words are harder for someone to read and understand quickly. The more long words you use, the less readable the text.

It's not about 'dumbing down' – most people just prefer to read Plain English. Why use a long word when a short one will do?

Example

- ▶ Don't forget your swim things, we want to spend the whole day at the beach.
- ▶ Remember your swimming paraphernalia, we're planning an expedition to the seaside for the duration of today.

Both say pretty much the same – but the second takes longer to read. It's harder to take in, and also much harder to remember.

When it comes to CVs, it's a reminder that long words don't make you sound better. By making your CV harder to read, they also tend to make you more forgettable. After reading the sentences below, look away for 30 seconds and then see which one you recall most of.

Example

- ▶ Outstanding sales professional accustomed to exceeding objectives at every opportunity, most evident when situations are challenging and require innovation and improvisation.
- ▶ Skilled salesperson, uses a creative approach and quick thinking to exceed targets.

SENTENCE LENGTH

Longer sentences are also harder to read and understand quickly. They tend to be more complex and may deal with more than one point or topic.

Example

Rather than:

▶ Sentences that are long tend to have lots of subclauses, which divide up the sentence and allow you to go off at a tangent and include unrelated concepts – a bit like the way my friends tend to talk when they drink too much beer (although I always stay sober as I'm driving) when we meet up on a Friday – and are far more complex to read and process than pure, short, single-concept sentences.

Try:

▶ Long sentences tend to have lots of subclauses. Subclauses divide up a sentence so you can cover more than one concept. My friends tend to talk in subclauses when they drink too much beer at our Friday meet-ups but I stay sober as I'm always driving. Complex subclauses are harder to read and process than short, simple sentences.

Rather than:

▶ Experienced doctor's receptionist respectful of patients' needs at all times – whether dealing with minor or major heath concerns sensitively, handling privately funded services such as life assurance reports and corporate medicals, or working with hospital and laboratory staff over patient test results – who follows procedures to ensure confidentiality is always maintained, and results gained quickly, in order that patients rarely complain (only twice in five years), which is down to my polite, calm and helpful demeanour.

Try:

▶ Experienced doctor's receptionist, careful to respect patients' needs.

- ▶ Handling minor and major health concerns sensitively and confidentially.
- ▶ Managing life assurance reports, corporate medicals and hospital test results promptly and discreetly.
- ▶ Gaining just two patient complaints in more than five years shows my polite, calm and helpful demeanour.

When reading longer sentences, you have to think more carefully:

- ▶ To whom (or what) is the writer referring in each subclause?
- ▶ Is the subclause related to the point made just before, or not?
- ▶ Does it actually make sense overall?

You may find you need to re-read sentences like this before they are fully clear. All this takes much longer and, again, makes them harder to remember.

Dos
- ▶ **Do** aim for short sentences about single points or topics.
- ▶ **Do** use short words.
- ▶ **Do** put different or unrelated concepts in separate sentences.

Don'ts
- ▶ **Don't** overcomplicate things with overformal (long) sentences.
- ▶ **Don't** try to sound more business-like by using bigger words.
- ▶ **Don't** use too much jargon, especially long-worded jargon.
- ▶ **Don't** now add to sentences that you've already refined.

Always
- ▶ **Always** read your CV out loud when checking readability. Do it more than once.
- ▶ **Always remember:** if you repeatedly stumble over any part, it's probably not very readable.
- ▶ **Always** double-check to see whether you have used over-formal language or too much jargon.
- ▶ **Always** try to use shorter words and sentences to say the same thing.

If you can pick up and read any part out loud without a hitch, it should be readable to most other people. Again, the proof is in the pudding – ask someone else to read it and ask what they think!

Quality control

Quality control is usually the final stage of checks or tests before a finished product is sent out to customers. In the same way, this is the final step for your CV content. And that means **final**.

Don't get into quality control until you are sure there are no more changes to be made, otherwise you are just wasting your time.

When you think you are done, close your CV and take a break. If you have written your CV by hand up to this point, now is the time to get it typed. Then, with a clear mind, go back and proofread it to check for any errors.

PROOFREADING

It is notoriously hard to proofread your own work, even if you are an English professor. That's because you know what you wrote or rather, you know what you intended to write. Your brain tends to fill in any gaps and skim over errors without realizing.

Ideal is asking a friend with a good eye for detail – and great English – to proofread it for you. They could spot something you have overlooked again and again.

If you can't ask someone else to help, then read it out loud to yourself, very slowly. Pretend it's the first time you've ever seen it. Read every part aloud: even your own name, address, phone number, email address and all dates. This really helps show up any errors.

Look out for:

- ▶ typos, for example, 1898 instead of 1998, manger instead of manager
- ▶ spelling mistakes, for example, it's negotiate (not negociate), professional (not proffesional)
- ▶ punctuation, for example, 'It's my dream' is correct, 'Its my dream' is not
- ▶ poor grammar, for example, 'Making sure budgets wasn't exceeded' (single vs. plural)
- ▶ inconsistencies, for example, Profiters R Us on page 1 and Profiteers R Us on page 2
- ▶ 'unintentionals', for example, 'Getting a rise out of the sales manager every six months'.

COMPUTER SPELL CHECKERS

Don't just rely on the computer's spell check to put everything right: it isn't able to understand the meaning of your words, and is therefore open to error.

Insight

Spell checkers don't pick up typos that are contextual errors, i.e. typos that also happen to be real words. Examples include manage and mange, account and count, know and now, as and has, for example: 'I mange all aspects of project planning and budgeting.'

When a spell check does suggest changing a word, think before you agree. Don't ever let the spell check run itself, especially with real names and places, or with foreign words. Depending on your software dictionary and what you've added to it over time, substitutions can be odd, funny or downright insulting.

Two different computers were used to spell check different letters going out to the same patient. The spell check was automatic:

▶ Mrs Halliwell was transformed into Mrs Halloween or Mrs Halitosis.
▶ Odstock Hospital became Woodstock Hospital or Odious Hospital.
▶ Dr De'Ath, already a difficult moniker for a medic, was the enchanting Dr Death in both.

During quality control if you find any mistakes that need correcting – a word, comma, space, bullet point, anything – then remember to do your quality control again afterwards.

It might seem like overkill but in the heat of last-minute changes, it's very easy to delete two words instead of one, ignore a missing phrase, mistype a date, misspell a name, or even add a random letter or symbol.

After all this hard work, your finished CV deserves to be completely error-free.

TEN THINGS TO REMEMBER

1 *Your CV needs to be legible, scannable and readable.*

2 *Legible text is large enough, well-formed and well-spaced.*

3 *Scannable text is logically broken up into labelled, manageable chunks.*

4 *Readable text uses simple words and short sentences as far as possible.*

5 *To check readability, read your whole CV out loud.*

6 *Reading your CV aloud ensures you are comfortable with the language.*

7 *Quality controlling your finished CV is essential before it is sent out.*

8 *Don't trust your computer's spell checker to do everything.*

9 *If you can't proofread well, ask a friend to do it.*

10 *Every time you change a targeted CV, save a copy.*

13

....

Format – factors to consider

In this chapter you will learn:
* **how to choose between digital and paper CVs**
* **about other non-standard CV formats and when to use them**

Whenever you have a choice and the job advert doesn't specify, send a paper CV.

_____

Why paper?

Most studies show it takes people longer to read from a screen than from a printed sheet, so make it quick and easy. Paper can even encourage a recruiter to take your CV away from their desk and read it elsewhere, even at home. Your CV is likely to be paid more attention under these circumstances.

Paper may cost a bit more than email, but it's worth it to make life easier for the recruiter. Of course, a paper CV is not welcome if you are specifically asked to submit by email.

Advantages of a paper CV:

▶ faster to read
▶ layout and text cannot be altered
▶ has a physical presence, is touchable
▶ can be read anywhere
▶ no compatibility issues

▶ it can't be 'unopenable' (unless you decide to superglue the envelope) so it's guaranteed to be right there in front of the recruiter's eyes, whereas if someone has a problem opening your digital CV file, they might not bother asking you to send it again – especially if lots of other CVs do open first time.

Disadvantages of a paper CV:

▶ more expensive
▶ tempting to print bulk copies (instead of tailoring each one)
▶ can get damaged
▶ untraceable if lost: recruiter can't go back and print another copy
▶ post is slower than email – not ideal if you're applying at the last minute.

PAPER CONSIDERATIONS

Question: What kind of paper, print and envelope should I use for my printed CV?

Answer:

▶ Good quality paper: ideally 120gsm weight and slightly textured.
▶ Very pale coloured paper: pale cream, pale blue or pale grey, with black text.
▶ Print your covering letter on the same paper stock as your CV.
▶ Unless requested, use paperclips instead of staples.
▶ A4 envelope (remember to use a 'large' stamp) – brown or white irrelevant.

WHY?

▶ Good quality paper is less likely to be damaged.
▶ Slightly textured paper feels nicer to hold in your hand.
▶ Black text on plain pastel paper is easiest to read, especially for people with dyslexia. Black text on white paper can cause more glare and makes a CV harder to read.
▶ Coloured text or brightly coloured paper is an absolute no-no.

- ▶ A4 envelopes are better than A5 or DL as you won't need to fold your CV. If you do fold it, it can be harder to:
  - ▷ do automated scanning
  - ▷ photocopy
  - ▷ stack in a pile of other CVs
  - ▷ file.
- ▶ This also applies to staples, which are awkward to remove for scanning, copying or filing.

When sending a paper CV ensure pages are clearly numbered and also named; then, if the sheets do get separated, it's easy to see which ones belong together.

Digital CVs

The standard format for creating a digital CV is Microsoft Word. It is simple to use, easily editable and every employer should be able to open and read a .doc or .docx file. Beware of creating very complex layouts with too many boxes, outlines or embedded images: these can change format when viewed on other people's computers.

Another way to email your CV is as an Adobe PDF file. Adobe Acrobat Reader software is free online and enables you to open a PDF. The great advantage of PDFs is their layout and appearance is fixed and can't change, no matter what computer they are viewed on.

Before emailing your CV, check the filename is appropriate and begins with your own name: e.g. GeorgeClooneyCV.docx. When recruiters receive 500 CV files, almost all entitled 'CV.docx', working through them becomes extremely awkward. They'll thank you for making things easy.

Insight

Make it easy for yourself too. Save each targeted CV carefully under an obvious filename. Was it GeorgeClooneyCV12 or

GeorgeClooneyCV13 you needed to email to Halfords? If it's saved as GeorgeClooneyCVHalfords.docx then there's less chance of you sending the wrong CV. Provided you named it properly in the first place!

Advantages of a digital CV:

- ▶ zero printing, stationery and postage costs
- ▶ quick to arrive: great for last-minute applications
- ▶ pages can't be lost
- ▶ simple to post on internet job sites
- ▶ can easily be shared with other interested recruiters
- ▶ return receipts can let you know when/if it's been read
- ▶ automated scanning for keywords is simple.

Disadvantages of a digital CV:

- ▶ can be shared/sent on without you knowing
- ▶ private details less likely to remain confidential
- ▶ file may get corrupted and be impossible to open
- ▶ file may not be compatible with other computers
- ▶ layout format may change when viewed on a different computer
- ▶ can only be read on a screen
- ▶ no physical qualities exist to help it stand out from other files.

Non-standard CV formats

This includes formats such as Video or Podcast CVs. Yes, there are more ways than 2D to get your message and selling points across. No, you don't have to (and shouldn't) try to be different just for the sake of it.

Alternative CV formats such as Video CVs are particularly appropriate for some industries, especially those focused on visual aspects such as entertainment, advertising, marketing, media, technology and design. While there is also an increasing number of people from more traditional business backgrounds exploring the video CV format, many employers may not have seen one before and would not expect to receive one. This could count for or against you.

Generally speaking, the advice is to use a CV format that will:

- ▶ be accepted by the employer, and
- ▶ give you the biggest advantage.

Nevertheless, there are some advantages to using a video CV. It is perfect for communicating a visual portfolio quickly and in parallel with other details. If relevant to the job you want, it's also an excellent opportunity to demonstrate your creativity and, if not, the novelty factor may help you stand out in sectors where video CVs are unusual.

However, the potential pitfalls may outweigh using this format for traditional sectors.

Adding a photograph to a CV is risky and not normally recommended, and the same proviso goes for video. Your appearance might distract people from your qualifications or even put them off. It is human nature to make assumptions about people based on their appearance alone. The watcher of your video may decide on your intelligence and likeability before you even open your mouth. You are also revealing information that could unconsciously be used to discriminate against you – age, ethnicity, for example – however hard the recipient tries not to.

Video needs to be really short and full of impact as it can't be skimmed through. Get straight to the point. How many busy recruiters would rather sit through the entire two to three minutes of video than take a few seconds to glean what they need from your written CV?

Just as for a written CV, style and presentation is all-important. When production or playback quality let you down, your video CV is effectively worthless. Unless you are a born performer you will likely need a lot of time, practice and decent equipment to do yourself justice. That doesn't mean don't bother, only that you should do it properly or not at all.

Many people recommend sending a video CV with their paper CV, but if this is the case, be sure your video CV adds more than just a view of your face and a sample of your voice. Reading your CV out on screen while the recruiter reads a copy of it more quickly and easily themselves is not going to capture the imagination. The same applies if your video is a voiceover for a PowerPoint presentation. If you send both formats, ensure your written CV stands alone on its own merits and think about using a video CV to enhance your appeal – the visual equivalent of a covering letter, giving your highlights with an insight into your presentation style. Or you could focus on illustrating and demonstrating your skills in the video CV, providing proof that backs up your written CV.

Video CVs may well become more popular, particularly with younger applicants more comfortable with this format, but until it's possible to scan through a video at high speed it's unlikely they will challenge the traditional CV for preferred format.

CVs for overseas applications

Just as different sectors have particular expectations of a CV, so do different countries. Rather than go into detail here, Chapter 18 directs you to online resources that will explain key changes you may need to make to your CV in terms of personal details, photographs, the importance of education and the overall chronology or structure.

Whoever the employer and wherever they are based, it never hurts to:

▶ choose one language (English or local) and stick to it throughout your CV
▶ place the most relevant parts at the beginning
▶ keep it brief and aim for a maximum of two pages.

The Europass CV format

This bears consideration if you are looking to live and work in Europe, for a European employer. If you aren't sure what format CV to send or how best to explain your qualifications, try the Europass website (more details in Chapter 18).

The Europass program was developed to try to make skills, experience and qualifications more transparent and meaningful to employers in other European countries. Europass CV templates exist online and can be filled in and saved in XML or PDF + XML format. The format is designed to be compatible with automated scanning systems and to be uploaded directly into standard European HR databases.

The online template can be filled in quite quickly if you keep your generic CV to hand. Once saved to your computer in XML format, you can upload and update it whenever you want. No copies are saved on the internet so it is a secure way of working.

The section on skills is quite useful, as it categorizes the different types of skill employers are interested in. Even if you don't use a Europass format, this might help you remember something useful to add into your generic CV.

You may not speak any other languages. If English is your first language you may be lucky in that often you won't need to. However, if you have learned one or more other languages, there is a simple Europass system for rating your ability to understand, speak and write in that language. This standardized system can be a useful way to show your language ability, even if you are writing a UK-only CV or choose not to use the full Europass format for a European application.

The CV template on the Europass site isn't quite as flexible as making your own: the order of information is predetermined and the layout is fixed. However, there is space for extra details and the style of writing is still unique to you. Depending on the job you want, it may be an advantage to use Europass. If you're still not sure, it's a useful process to go through – and you can always ask prospective employers if they welcome Europass CVs.

EUROPASS CERTIFICATE SUPPLEMENTS

Also useful are the Europass certificate supplements for your qualifications such as City and Guilds. These supplements, available from most examining bodies, help explain to a European employer exactly what the course is called (translated), what it entailed, the skills required to pass, and the jobs for which you are now qualified. These supplements should be used in conjunction with the relevant UK certificate, not on their own.

TEN THINGS TO REMEMBER

1 *Make life as easy as possible for the recruiter.*

2 *Send a paper CV if possible; you have more control over it.*

3 *Black text on quality, pale-coloured paper is the safest bet.*

4 *Use the same paper stock for CVs, letters and additional sheets.*

5 *Carefully save targeted digital CVs under self-explanatory filenames.*

6 *Check that CVs for foreign employers meet local requirements: ask if you need to.*

7 *Europass CV format is worth exploring for international applications.*

8 *Use alternative format CVs if they are appropriate and enhance your application.*

9 *Only send out your CV, whatever the format, once it is finished to a high degree.*

10 *If you can't finish your CV to a high quality by yourself, ask for help.*

Part six
Using it properly

By now you have prepared, written, refined and targeted your CV, and perfected its presentation. Friends, family, colleagues or recruiters have given you feedback along the way. Congratulations – it is now finished! Print a copy of your CV and look at it with pride.

And, of course, double check one last time to ensure there aren't any mistakes ...

Strangely it's the next stage that some people find hardest of all: sending your CV out. Maybe that's because once you send it, you can't take it back. After all this time spent making it as good as possible, it can be hard to admit it's ready to go.

Constant rewriting can be an unconscious delaying tactic and may be a sign you're still worried what people will think of it. But however good your CV is, it can't get you an interview while it's sitting on your desk – and it certainly can't post itself. If you're guilty of serial editing, try setting yourself a deadline for sending your application (aim for at least one week before the closing date, not the last possible day) and then stick to it.

When you do send off your targeted CV, there are three further things you'll need to consider:

- ▶ what should accompany it? (covering letter, email, application form?)
- ▶ can you follow through? (can your interview be as strong as your CV?)
- ▶ how do you keep it fresh? (can you avoid updating it if you don't need to change job?).

Some useful guidelines for the above are suggested in the following chapters.

14

Complementing your CV: covering letters and application forms

In this chapter you will learn:
- *the purpose of a covering letter or email and what it should contain*
- *how to use CVs with application forms and statements*

Covering letters

It's rare that a recruiter opens an envelope to find nothing but a CV inside. As a rule, a CV is always sent with a one-page covering letter or email that:

- ▶ names the role you are applying for
- ▶ highlights why you would be perfect for this role at this company
- ▶ encourages the recipient to read your CV and invite you for interview.

It's fair to say that this letter is, in many ways, even more important than your CV. A good letter guarantees that someone will at least skim through your CV. Dull, irrelevant or badly-written letters beg to go straight in the bin – swiftly followed by your CV, however good it was.

Your covering letter needs to seduce the reader. It should take them by the hand, pat the seat and say: 'Come and sit down. I've got an amazing CV for you to read. Look – this person has everything you could possibly want, all you need to do is see that for yourself.' Once they start to read, they'll be hooked.

Letters that do the literary equivalent of shrugging their shoulders and saying: 'Here, have a quick peek at this CV. It's quite good, you might even like some of it,' are not doing as much as they should to help you. Worse still, if they mutter: 'It's a lot to ask but I'm hoping something in this CV might just catch your eye if you have the patience to give it a proper read', then all your time spent learning to write an amazing CV has been wasted.

What type of covering letter should you use?

Many people feel that you should have a different type of covering letter for each type of application. Job adverts in the press vs. online job adverts, employer vs. recruitment agency adverts, responsive vs. speculative letters, for example. However, with the possible exception of purely speculative applications, every covering letter or email basically needs to say the same things. It's how you say them that matters.

What to include in a covering letter

You can include up to six points, ideally all fitting on one side of paper. Have a separate short paragraph for each.

1 Say clearly why you are sending your CV
Are you:
▶ answering an advert?
▶ writing speculatively, to ask if there are any opportunities for someone with your skills?
▶ sending a CV because a mutual contact suggested you do so?

2 Very briefly, say why you are an ideal person for this/a job

▶ What skills and experience do you have that would be useful to them?
▶ What would help you do this job better than others might be able to?
▶ Direct them to your enclosed/attached CV to see proof of this, and more.

3 State why you would like to work for this particular company
It might be due to:
▶ reputation
▶ culture
▶ performance
▶ feedback from acquaintances who work there
▶ personal interest in/passion for their products
▶ location
▶ opportunities for progression
▶ concern for the environment
▶ any other sensible reason you can think of.

4 Add any other important details that aren't already in your CV
You may wish to:
▶ explain that you are about to relocate or are willing to do so if needed
▶ give details of your current salary – only if specifically asked for
▶ confirm that you have a valid driving licence
▶ mention a relevant training course or qualification that you are due to start very soon
▶ be creative and add a testimonial from one of your appraisals or references.

5 Say what response you would like from the recipient
This might be:
▶ an interview for the job advertised (do mention if you are unavailable, for example, away on holiday)
▶ an initial conversation with someone about potential opportunities
▶ written details of current vacancies

- ▶ your CV to be kept on file
- ▶ your CV to be forwarded/recommended for consideration, if sent to a personal contact
- ▶ anything else you would like them to do.

6 End your letter with any action you intend to take (if you do intend to)

Let them know that you:

- ▶ are going to telephone next week to check your application has arrived safely
- ▶ will wait to hear back from them
- ▶ welcome the chance to discuss further at interview
- ▶ look forward to meeting them.

Example

Good

I'm writing to apply for the role of restaurant manager at Munch Soho.

I have seven years' experience running restaurant franchises and my inspired team leadership and enthusiasm creates a great working environment. I'd welcome the challenge of managing a larger restaurant, and I can relocate to central London immediately if desired. I look forward to discussing further at interview; I'm on holiday from 13–20 September.

Tony Bellifull

All the key points are included, but there are a few things that need to be added:

- ▶ where you saw the job advert (recruiters love to know how effective each ad is)
- ▶ more evidence of skills mentioned: concrete examples
- ▶ refer the reader to the CV you've included
- ▶ holiday notice seems a little abrupt at the end.

Better

I'm writing in response to your recent *Times* advert for a restaurant manager at the new Munch Soho.

I have seven years' experience running successful restaurant franchises: Zaza's in Uxbridge and more recently Babel in Brighton. My inspired team leadership and enthusiasm creates a great working environment, as you can see from my CV.

I'm now looking to manage a larger restaurant, with scope for progression. Munch in Soho would be perfect, especially with its strong focus on healthy foods. I can relocate to central London immediately if desired.

I look forward to discussing further at interview; please note I'm on holiday from 13–20 September and won't be available during that time.

Yours sincerely,

Tony Bellifull

This is an improvement, but you could make some further refinements:

▶ Be specific about the date of the advert you are replying to.
▶ Sell yourself harder: mention more skills, offer tasters of the proof in your CV.
▶ See whether including a quoted reference or testimonial might make you stand out.

Best

I'm writing to apply for the role of restaurant manager at Munch Soho, as advertised in *The Times* on Sunday 16 February.

Seven years' experience setting up and running profitable restaurants, firstly Zaza's in Uxbridge and more recently Babel in Brighton, has fine-tuned my commercial awareness. Inspired team leadership and enthusiasm make my restaurants an attractive place to work or eat and, as you will see from my CV, this has kept staff turnover low and customers coming back.

(Contd)

To apply my skills at a larger restaurant, within a fast-growing chain where there is scope for progression to regional manager, is my ideal next step. The opening of the largest Munch restaurant in Soho would be perfect, especially with its strong focus on healthy foods – a real passion of mine. I am able to relocate to central London immediately if needed.

My previous manager described me as having 'a potent mix of marketing skills based on astute customer insight': I'd love the chance to elaborate on the added value I can bring to this role and the all-important marketing of your new restaurant.

Please note I'm on holiday from 13–20 September but would be available for interview at any other time.

Yours sincerely,

Tony Bellifull

Don't just repeat, enhance

Don't copy chunks of your CV into a letter. It'll be easy to see when skim reading your CV whether you are simply reiterating what's in the covering letter without adding anything new. If this is the case, it's unlikely your CV will be read much further. Your covering letter should distill down your CV into the three or four most relevant points.

However, the names you give the skills and experience in your covering letter should be identical to those in your CV, and both should reflect the advert wording in case automated scanning is used. In the restaurant manager example above, these key words might be:

- ▶ 'seven years' experience'
- ▶ 'commercial awareness'
- ▶ 'profitable'
- ▶ 'leadership'
- ▶ 'enthusiasm'.

Nothing else should be identical: the letter is merely the taster, and the CV is where your specific examples are given.

How you describe skills and experience in a letter should differ from your CV in several ways:

1 Use sentences, not bullet points
Summarize the detail in your CV to make it more persuasive in a letter – but don't add too many words! The same CV rules apply to a covering letter: keep it relevant and concise.

2 Mention new examples or achievements that show off your skills
If your letter complements or mentions your 'proof of skills', this strengthens your CV further. Any good examples that didn't make it into your targeted CV could be used instead in the covering letter to help you avoid repeating yourself.

When the only remaining examples from your generic CV are quite weak, then play safe: stick to the examples given in your targeted CV – just summarize them differently.

3 Use references, appraisals and other reports creatively
A brief testimonial can be very powerful when used properly and a covering letter or email is the ideal place to make it stand out.

Look back through your paperwork from jobs, or even school and university. Do you have an appraisal with a particularly glowing compliment about your skills? A letter or email commending your performance, recommending you for promotion or congratulating you for a particular achievement? A 'standard' reference letter from a former employer? A personal note from a tutor or teacher regarding a particularly outstanding piece of work?

Select one phrase from one of these sources that is particularly relevant to the job you're applying for and add it into your covering letter, in quotation marks, as another source of proof. You can either build it into one of your paragraphs or, if particularly relevant, position it as a standalone quote. For an employer to read that another employer has appreciated the benefits of your skills can be a strong and memorable reinforcement of your claims.

Like the certificates for qualifications, keep all your documentation safe so you can provide proof of what you are saying. If not clear, make a note of who made the comment. When invited to interview it may help to take along the page or excerpt that contains the quote, just in case you are asked about it. By all means take more examples, if you have them, as backup. Just make sure (especially if you are using an old appraisal) that there is nothing damning on the same page as your star quote!

If your quote comes from an existing personal or professional reference, do let them know that you are using it and ideally send them a copy to refresh their memory: they may well have forgotten what they said, which doesn't look good if they are questioned about it.

4 Target your letter just as much as, if not more, than your CV

One of the key things that should stand out in your covering letter is not just what you have to offer, but why you want to work in **this role** and for **this company**.

This is particularly important if you are applying speculatively – show the reader that you've done your homework and know exactly what you want. Some targeted information may be in your Objective already, but you can be much more precise in a letter.

If your CV doesn't include an objective, then the covering letter is your only chance to communicate your ambitions and sell the 'fit' between you and the company.

The more targeted your CVs and letters become, the more care you will need to take to ensure you always start a new CV or letter from a generic template, not the previous targeted version.

Insight

If you are sending out several applications for similar roles, be VERY careful to check any company names throughout your documents before you send them out. Make sure every part of your application (CV objective, letter address, letter content, envelope) mentions the same company name.

Applying to Wilkinson Sword saying you've always wanted to work for Gillette might be vaguely amusing for the reader, but is not likely to put you at the top of the shortlist. Nor would claiming lifelong brand loyalty to Kit Kats on a letter to the Human Resources department at Masterfoods.

Covering emails

Ideally a covering email can be read on one screen without having to scroll down. In most respects it should be exactly the same as the equivalent covering letter:

▶ Use the same language, layout and content as a printed letter, although you can delete postal address details and dates as this is tagged automatically.
▶ Put the vacancy you are applying for in the subject line of the email to make it easy for the recipient, especially if it's a recruitment agency handling lots of vacancies.

Speculative cover letters/emails

Generally speaking, speculative applications are best sent by post and not by email.

With mountains of spam received every day, emails are (thankfully) very quick and easy to ignore. However, this means that the recipient may never get further than the subject line of your email before clicking 'Delete'. A creative subject line may help, but only if the person you sent it to is not overloaded with work when they receive it.

The chances are that most people, however busy, will at some point open an envelope that is addressed to them. For senior management, at least their personal assistant should. This gives you more chance of getting your letter in front of their eyes. While hard copies admittedly cost more to send out, this investment – of both your time and your money – is less likely to be dismissed out of hand.

If you have limited resources, use them wisely: make fewer speculative applications to better-researched companies with which you are a better match, rather than spamming as many employers as possible in the hope of getting a 'hit'.

Targeting your covering letter

Your starting point for a targeted CV is your generic CV, which you edit according to a specific opportunity – ideally based on the job advert if there is one.

Your starting point for a targeted covering letter is your targeted CV. There should be no such thing as a generic covering letter.

The following example for a retail manager shows the steps you should take and in which order.

Example

Step 1

Sample employment entry from a generic CV:

Jun 2007–Jan 2010   Department Manager,
                           LuxeLuxe, Manchester
One-of-a-kind department store: a reputation for luxury
and over 1m visitors per year

▶ Managing all aspects of Gifts & Treats, the largest
  department in the store.
▶ Motivating a 23-strong team to delight customers with
  gorgeous gifts and great service.
▶ Raising customer satisfaction levels to 98 per cent by
  developing staff product knowledge.
▶ Introducing a commission-based incentive which
  increased sales by 23 per cent pre-Christmas.
▶ Driving footfall at non-seasonal times by devising new
  gift 'occasions' and promotions.
▶ Using innovative sales techniques to make shopping fun
  and generate repeat business, such as digital 'wish lists',
  'sent from' notes and 'my first' occasions.
▶ Bringing in brand new customers with 'entry-level'
  pricing on selected quality gift ranges.

Step 2

Sample entry from a targeted CV:

You want to be floor manager at a London department
store. Research suggests sales are falling in the current
downturn. The last four bullet points are your most
relevant, and you want to point out that you already manage
a sizeable team. So you condense the first bullets and

(Contd)

remove others, one of which you expand in your covering letter: innovative sales techniques, as this merits the detail and will help you stand out.

Jun 2007–Jan 2010   Department Manager, LuxeLuxe, Manchester

One-of-a-kind department store with a reputation for luxury and over 1m visitors per year.
Managing the 23-strong team in Gifts & Treats, the largest department in the store.

▶ Introducing a commission-based incentive which increased sales by 23% pre-Christmas.
▶ Driving footfall at non-seasonal times by devising new gift 'occasions' and promotions.
▶ Bringing in brand new customers with 'entry-level' pricing on selected quality gift ranges.

Step 3

Sample targeted covering letter:

Address 1
Address 2
Address 3

Ms Rosa Recruta
Address 1
Address 2
Address 3

Date: 23 January 2010

Dear Ms Recruta,

I am writing in response to your *Telegraph* advert dated 18 January 2010 for a Floor Manager at Coleridges.

Skilled at managing large teams, you will also see from my CV that I employ innovative techniques to maintain staff motivation and year-round sales in a traditionally seasonal department. For example, during 2009 I introduced the highly successful digital 'wish list': photographing customers in store with aspirational products and creating online wish lists for friends and family to view – and even contribute funds to – online. This was extremely effective in attracting customers during the summer, tying them to a particular product and ensuring the sale remained with our store.

Having proved my ability at department level, my ambition is to excel at floor level. I would love to do this at Coleridges, a store I have admired since childhood and one whose traditional approach would be complemented by my creative approach to sales.

I will call next week to confirm receipt of my application and to find out when might be a suitable time to discuss my application further.

Yours sincerely,

Burcin Baskit

Step 4

If needed, convert to sample targeted covering email:

Recipient: rosa_recruta@coleridges.com
Subject: Vacancy – Coleridges Floor Manager

Dear Ms Recruta,

I am applying for the above position advertised in *The Telegraph* on 18 January 2010.

(Contd)

Skilled at managing large teams, you will also see from my attached CV that I employ innovative techniques to maintain staff motivation and year-round sales in a traditionally seasonal department. For example, during 2009 I introduced the highly successful digital 'wish list': photographing customers in store with aspirational products and creating online wish lists for friends and family to view – and even contribute funds to – online. This was extremely effective in attracting customers during the summer, tying them to a particular product and ensuring the sale remained with our store.

Having proved my ability at department level, my ambition is to excel at floor level. I would love to do this at Coleridges, a store I have admired since childhood and one whose traditional approach would be complemented by my creative approach to sales.

I will call next week to confirm receipt of my application and to find out when might be a suitable time to discuss my application further.

Yours sincerely,

Burcin Baskit

Application forms

Quite often employers will ask for a CV to be sent with their application form. In this case, you should still send a short covering letter detailing which job you are applying for, why this employer and why you'd be great, but take care not to duplicate information that is given in either your CV or your application form.

It might seem odd to send both, especially when many of the questions on the application form are answered in your CV. Application forms are often asked for because CVs can vary dramatically in style and content. As a CV writer, you are entitled to highlight whichever points you want – and to play down any parts you don't feel proud of. This can make CVs quite hard to compare. An application form can be much more specific, ensuring everyone submits similar information and often asking questions way beyond the remit of any CV. Questions on application forms may test your knowledge, how you think, or your likely ability to handle specific challenges at work.

Insight

Always make and keep a copy of any application forms you fill out. Nothing is more unsettling before a job interview than being unable to remember what you sent. If you create a CV, a letter or an application form on screen, save a copy under a separate name so you don't overwrite it with anything else.

If you fill out a paper application, copy it twice. Before you start, copy the blank form so you can practise filling it out and, when you have finished, copy the final version before sending.

When filling in an application form, keep your generic CV open next to you:

▶ **Filling out the basics, like education and dates, is much quicker.**

All relevant details are in one place so you can just copy them across.

▶ **It's easier to answer questions about how or when you have shown particular skills.**

You thought of all your examples already when writing your generic CV.

Don't copy word for word, though, if you're also asked to send your CV. Try to use different examples to those given in your CV, if you have enough strong examples.

▶ **You might want to go back and tweak your targeted CV.**

Let's say the application form asks for lots of detail in one area, but you only touched lightly on this in your CV. It's never too late to go back and target your CV more effectively: just remember to proofread it again once you've made changes.

▶ **You may wish to update your generic CV.**

If a new question on an application form inspires you to come up with a great point or example that you hadn't thought of before, add it into your generic CV in the appropriate place. You never know when it might come in useful on a future CV or covering letter.

▶ **Both documents should be consistent.**

It doesn't look good if, for example, the dates of your qualifications on your CV and application form don't agree, especially when you are claiming attention to detail as one of your strengths.

Insight

Once you have finished your letter or application form, whether on paper or online, go through the same quality checks before sending as you would with your CV. Ensure there are no spelling mistakes or other errors: these make such a bad first impression. If you're not much of a proofreader, ask a friend who is to check it for you.

Personal statements or competency statements

These are terms you may also come across when applying for jobs. You may be asked to submit a personal statement or competency statement – with or without your CV.

Any good CV will already contain the basic ingredients for this statement. Unless instructed otherwise, it is normally a summary of the fields in which you are experienced, proof of your skills and competencies, and the direction you wish to head in your career.

To start creating your statement, try combining the Profile and Objective from your targeted CV – but of course don't leave it worded exactly the same if you are submitting your CV at the same time. Some rephrasing will be needed, with possibly more detail.

Personal or competency statements, like CVs and covering letters, should be written with a specific role and employer in mind. This ensures you focus on the competencies and skills most relevant to that job and that company, especially if you have limited space.

If the statement needs to be a specific length, edit it down or up from your starting point accordingly. Be as concise as you can when editing down, and when you really can't make it any shorter, think about deleting the least relevant points.

Insight

Editing up means adding relevant examples as proof of your skills, not using extra words (fluff) to say exactly the same thing as you did before.

Statements can be written as one chunk of prose, or split into shorter paragraphs, or even divided up under individual competency or skill headings. If you are not given specific guidelines, the choice is yours – but bear in mind that one solid chunk of prose can look off-putting.

The best advice is to try laying it out in several ways to see what looks right. Paragraphs are likely to work best for shorter statements, while breaking up text with headings would make a longer statement more readable.

TEN THINGS TO REMEMBER

1 *Your covering letter creates your first impression: ensure it's a positive one.*

2 *The primary aim of a covering letter or email is to get your CV read.*

3 *Covering letters should be maximum one page long and include six key points.*

4 *Don't repeat large chunks of your CV in a covering letter.*

5 *Quote references or letters of commendation in your letter as extra proof.*

6 *Spend as much effort targeting covering letters as you do CVs.*

7 *Refer to your generic CV when writing application forms or statements.*

8 *If an application form generates a good example, add it into your generic CV.*

9 *Ensure covering letters/emails are mistake-free before you send them.*

10 *Keep copies of everything you send to each employer, clearly named for ease.*

15

Living up to your great CV
at interview

In this chapter you will learn how to:
- **build your confidence before interview**

OK, so you've finally finished your CV and your application.
Now all the careful presentation and positive spin is complete,
you have another fear: *Does it all make you sound too good?*

When you spend so long writing about how good you are, this can
become a problem ... you start to feel as if you can't possibly live
up to it at interview.

Of course you can! Here's why:

You wrote it yourself

Being able to live up to and talk confidently about the skills you've
put down on paper has got to be the biggest benefit to writing your
own CV. After all, you've:

- done all the background work
- thought carefully about all the times you've shown your skills
- put these skill examples into clear, short sentences
- picked the most relevant sentences and included them in a
  carefully targeted CV
- made sure you're comfortable with the words you've used

► read it out loud so it feels easy and familiar when you talk about it.

If you didn't write your CV yourself, there is a risk it will contain impressive-sounding words that you don't really relate to. For example, would you ever say the following sentence out loud?

'Maximizing departmental productivity through visionary leadership aligned to strategic objectives'?

OK, a few people might. But be honest – would you? Even if you would, it's a hard sentence to repeat confidently under the pressure of an interview.

'Building motivation by showing everyone in my department how their actions impact the whole company.'

This might be a more natural way to put it. You can remember this second sentence more easily, and are more likely to be able to say it in front of an interviewer without stumbling.

When your CV and the way you speak at interview are really mismatched, a competent interviewer will assume you probably didn't write your own CV. They might wonder why.

If you did get a professional CV writing service to provide your generic CV, they should tweak it for you until you are happy. But you should still ask for it as an electronic file, so you can then make any changes to the wording that will help you sound more natural, more like yourself. It also means you can target your CV properly.

You have pulled together proof of everything you claim

Keep a copy of your generic CV as well as your targeted CV and covering letter, and any application form, and refer to them all.

You can do this before and during an interview. It can help to keep all the details you might need at the top of your mind (or on your lap) including extra examples of skills shown that are not in your CV. It will also remind you exactly what you told the company when you applied. When you're making a lot of applications, this is important.

You should find that, having thought long and hard about your skill examples, they come more easily to mind when you are asked about them. This will make your answers more assured, helping you to appear more confident – even if you don't always feel it inside.

You have worked on your positive spin to cover problem areas

Spending time thinking about the areas you aren't so happy with in order to write about them positively on your CV should pay dividends when you get to interview. Even things that didn't make it onto your final CV should still have been captured on your generic CV, along with a well thought out and positive story.

It may help to re-read your generic CV and your positive stories before each interview. Then, having taken the time to convince yourself why:

- ▶ you decided that working would be more valuable than finishing that college course
- ▶ the things you achieved during your time between jobs are so useful to this employer
- ▶ you think your voluntary work would be so beneficial to this role
- ▶ it took you some time to find your first job
- ▶ you have hopped around from company to company

you should find positive spin is becoming a more natural way of thinking about things.

When you're questioned by an interviewer about something you used to feel let you down, all this preparation should help you answer with more confidence. Better still, let it give you the confidence to raise some of the trickier issues yourself that can't be avoided, and that way stay more in control of your interview.

You've been honest

Above all else, you can always live up to your CV if you've been honest.

ONE THING TO REMEMBER

▶ Re-read your generic CV and positive stories to bolster your confidence at interview.

16

CV maintenance

In this chapter you will:
- **understand why keeping your CV fresh is so important**
- **follow the checklist to regularly update your CV**

However you prepared your CV and got it ready to use, whether it was all your own work or done with help from friends or a professional CV writer, don't just say 'thank goodness that's over' once you get the job you are after. A CV should not be chucked into a drawer or archived on your computer as soon as you open the champagne, only to be left gathering dust until you suddenly need it again.

Your CV is the key to all sorts of opportunities, and to some extent can determine your career success and earning potential. It has the power to fundamentally change your life and should be treated accordingly.

Your CV is alive

Think of your CV as a puppy. Or kitten, if you're a cat person.

When your CV is young, you adore it. You lavish attention on it, you pick it up, stroke it and show it proudly to other people.

When it becomes old, you take it for granted and don't fuss over it any more.

If you ignore your CV and leave it shut away for long periods of time, it will quickly start to look scruffy. Granted, it won't pee on your carpet or chew the sofa (pity, as that would be a great incentive), but it's guaranteed to take much longer to respond to you when you do finally pay it some attention.

To keep a CV happy, you need to regularly check on it: groom it, feed it, and clean it out. It needs your love.

OK, that's about as far as this analogy will go, but hopefully it's made the point. CVs need to be checked more than just every few years when you apply for another job.

Regular CV checkups

Ideally, you should re-read (and add to) your generic CV a minimum of every six months. More often is fine; by all means update it as often as there is a change to make.

Current examples of all your skills are quicker and easier to add if you do it regularly. Thinking of good examples a year or two down the line can be very hard; if you lose your job and need your CV ready straight away, it can be even harder. A regular refresh means you can delete obsolete examples and remove any out of date or irrelevant information.

Revisiting your CV every few months also helps you to keep better tabs on the new skills and qualifications you are adding. If you haven't put anything new into your CV for six months or a year, maybe it's about time to look into that training course you were thinking about, to ask for more responsibility, to go for promotion – or even to find a new job.

CV update checklist

If you are employed and lucky enough to stay that way, still put aside time to update your generic CV at least every six months, and whenever there is a change in your career. This update should take three or four hours at most, probably a lot less if your job has stayed the same. That's just eight hours a year spent improving your chances of getting a job interview when you really need or want one – more than worth it, surely?

If you are unemployed and unlucky enough to still be that way, try putting aside time every month – away from specific applications – to think about and update your generic CV. Instead of taking recent skill examples from work, take them from your personal life, voluntary work, interests or training courses.

Here's what to check and update as needed:

1 **Contact details**: have you moved, changed your mobile, or got a new email address? Have you changed your name after getting married – or divorced?

2 **Profile**: are you still doing the same job, or has it changed? If it hasn't changed, is the emphasis different, do you have experience in a new sector, or with any new systems? Do you have any new qualifications or skills you can highlight here?

3 **Objective**: leave this if you don't know, but it can be helpful to have a generic objective that shows your next career move. Every six months it reminds you where you want to be/what you want to be doing, or you can change it to something new.

4 **Employment History**: have you changed your employer or changed your role while still working for this employer:
   ▷ Do you have any extra responsibility?
   ▷ Has your team grown?

- ▷ Have you taken on or completed any projects during this time?
- ▷ Did you meet your targets this month/quarter/year?
- ▷ Have you won any awards?
- ▷ Are there any good examples of you showing your existing skills?
- ▷ Have you gained any new skills, and if so what examples can you give?
- ▷ Are there any things you can now delete or, if you don't want to lose them totally, 'grey out'?
- ▷ Does your work experience or job shadowing five years ago still need a mention?

Keep old examples of work experience only if you developed or showed a skill that you have no recent examples of, or you intend to go back into the industry you were working in at the time. E.g. you worked as bar staff and want to get into on licence sales, or you worked in an equestrian centre and want to be fundraising manager for a horse charity.

5 **Education/Qualifications/Training**: while your past education is hopefully accurate and therefore fixed, have you any qualifications or further training to add? Either here or in a Further Training section, for example, Health and Safety in the Workplace? Project Management course? Bookkeeping? Presentation Skills? Mathematics GCSE?

Is there anything no longer relevant, like details of GCSEs if you have a degree and work experience? Keep them by all means, but grey them out. Anything that is no longer current can also be greyed out, for example an instructor qualification that needs to be kept up to date but hasn't.

6 **Professional memberships**: for example, if you are now a fully accredited accountant or engineer, or became a member of any professional or trade body, or have joined an association for instructors, add the details here. Include the date from which your membership or accreditation is valid, the level you hold (such as junior member, associate member, full member) and the full name of the organization.

7 **Further skills**: have you lived abroad, started or completed a language course, or taken a language exam? Update your proficiency in this language. Have you been trained in using spreadsheets, databases or studied computer programming? Add these to your IT skills. Did you learn how to use a CNC machine, qualify as an MOT examiner, do a First Aid at Work Certificate or gain a forklift licence?

8 **Interests**: are these all still current or, despite listing marathon running as an interest, did you do your last marathon years ago? If yes, with no running events since, it's time to replace it with something you've done more regularly or recently.

If you did a scuba diving course last month, started coaching a junior football team, or joined a film club, add it in. If you really haven't got anything to say here or it is all old news (activities you haven't done this year) then grey everything out. This gives you two options: to leave Interests out of your next targeted CV, or to be inspired and take up something new to fill the gap. It doesn't have to cost money.

Insight

Nervous about losing information that might turn out to be relevant in future? Use grey font for older or weaker information in your generic CV so that it fades into the background, without deleting it completely. If your generic CV gets too long, try saving it under a new name and deleting any grey text: you can always refer to an older file if needed.

Incorporate feedback

You don't have to ask for feedback on your generic CV every six months, unless you want to, of course – and your contacts are extremely understanding. However, you should always get feedback if you can on a targeted CV before you send it out – and afterwards if possible.

Whenever you get feedback, don't just update the targeted CV. If you think it is sound advice from a trusted source, update your generic CV at the same time. Add notes in a different colour if you think the feedback applies only to a particular role or industry; change the actual text if it's a universal comment and one that you agree with.

It is important only to make changes you agree with: each person will have a different, usually subjective, opinion. CVs are like Marmite – aspects that some people loathe, others will love. Don't feel you need to bend with the wind by incorporating every single comment you get, however contradictory.

If you aren't chosen for interview, it's worth making a quick call to see if you can find out why. Take great care not to sound defensive and make it clear you are merely trying to improve your CV, not having a go at someone for not asking you to interview! Not all employers will have the time or inclination to be helpful – and many will have already binned your CV by this point – but some might give you valuable feedback, so it's always worth making a polite call if you can. Nothing ventured, nothing gained.

Recruitment agencies especially are worth calling: don't just ask for feedback on your CV but also check whether there are any other positions they could put you forward for.

If you get the interview and are then offered the job and accept it, that's great. But don't pass up on yet another great opportunity for feedback. You'll probably get the most detailed answer of all from a new employer and/or boss as to what they liked or didn't like about your CV, and your interview style. Ask as soon as you can, so it's fresh in their mind as well as yours. Be sure to note their comments in your generic CV and bear them in mind when it comes to your next application – especially if you apply for a promotion or new role internally.

Be prepared

Boy Scouts and Girl Guides may have years to go before they need a CV, but they have the right idea: Be prepared. In an uncertain climate, you need to be ready to act fast.

However great you may be in your current role, when that stomach-dropping redundancy letter falls on your desk and you're up against 50 similarly-qualified colleagues to find a new job as of Monday, you'll be glad you were better prepared than they were for the task.

The same applies in positive situations, for example, when you're introduced to a company director late on a Friday night and discover he needs to fill an urgent vacancy, and would consider you if only you could email your CV to him at home by Saturday morning. Trying to write an inspired CV at midnight (or worse, at 7 a.m. with a hangover) isn't the best start, but if your generic CV is up to date then you only need to edit.

Being prepared might not earn you a CV-writing badge, but you can take comfort in knowing that you are ready for any opportunity that comes along. An effective, targeted CV takes a fraction of the time to prepare and send when your generic CV is bang up to date.

TEN THINGS TO REMEMBER

1 *A job takes eight hours a day: just eight hours a year could help you land the right one.*

2 *Don't ignore your CV just because you are happy at work right now.*

3 *Add new skills, proofs and achievements to your generic CV when they happen.*

4 *Describing recent examples is easier than remembering old ones.*

5 *Pull out and check your CV at least every six months.*

6 *Update basics like contact details as well as Employment History.*

7 *Generic CVs can be a barometer for professional development and career ambitions.*

8 *Re-writing a CV under pressure is harder than editing an up-to-date generic one.*

9 *Cutting corners on applications is more tempting if your CV needs lots of work.*

10 *Always try to ask for feedback on your CV, whether it was successful or not.*

Part
seven
Further help

There may be times when you look at your CV, however well polished it may be, and sigh.

It might be the first time you've ever written one; it might be the fiftieth time you've updated it. But deep down, you know it's not as good as it needs to be for the job you want and nothing you can honestly say is going to make it look better.

This is not about writing style, but about content, or a lack of it.

Part of the process of writing your CV should involve taking a good look at your skills and abilities. Consider whether there is anything more you can do to improve your chances of getting the interview and job you want. This is very pertinent if you hope for a change of career.

The next chapter covers ways you can try to improve a CV lacking in content, while the final chapter directs you to a range of further resources you might find useful.

17

Enhancing your employability – when nothing else works

In this chapter you will learn:
* **how to add to your skills when refining your CV alone is not enough**

Room for improvement

If you go through your generic CV every few months, you will usually discover a few niggles. Those parts that, every time you read them, you wish looked a bit better.

▶ The lack of industry experience that every job you'd like insists upon.
▶ Public speaking skills you don't have.
▶ Equipment or software you've never learned how to use.
▶ French stuck at GCSE level for a decade that is no use in your business.
▶ The ever-increasing amount of time you have been unemployed.

Whatever the niggle may be, don't just try to wish it away – or worse, lie. If there is something you could do to make your CV look better and give you more of a chance of getting to interview, why not do it?

Getting in early

It's never too early to write your first CV. Whether you're at school doing GCSEs next year, or A levels after that, or you are just starting further education, write it today. Yes, it's going to look pretty empty in places, but that's just what you need at this stage.

The gaps in your early CV might help you decide how to spend some of your time over the next year or two, if you're serious about wanting a job when you finish your education. That's not to say you should live your whole life by what will look good on your CV. But when things are tough and more people than ever are out of work, thinking about how your CV looks is something best done sooner.

The job market is already very competitive. Landing your first job with no experience can seem impossible. If you see a big gap in your CV now, start thinking how to close it.

The following pointers apply to improving your CV at various stages in your career:

START YOUNG

Some larger companies may prefer not to employ under-16s and so may require a national insurance number on your application, but there are many other jobs you can do before then. Types of work under-16s can legally do include:

- ▶ shelf stacking and other shop work
- ▶ washing hair or cleaning up in a hair salon
- ▶ car washing (by hand, on a private basis, not as part of a commercial operation)
- ▶ serving or clearing in a café or restaurant
- ▶ working in an office
- ▶ reception work
- ▶ domestic work in hotels and motels
- ▶ farm-related work, fruit picking or gardening.

Under-16s can't legally work in most higher-risk environments, which usually rules out things like heavy machinery, kitchens, chemicals, alcohol, or adult-oriented work.

If you can pick up babysitting work from friends and family, go for it. It might not seem very business-oriented, but it shows that other people think you are reliable, trustworthy and responsible enough to look after their children – all of which are valuable qualities in any employee.

Try to take a long-term view: some experience and a decent reference from any employer will give you a huge advantage when you leave school compared to those who haven't thought about their CV at all. Even if it's not your ideal career and you're not earning enough to shout about, it will pay off one day. At the very least it will give you a better chance of securing a better paid job doing work that interests you.

DON'T DISMISS VOLUNTARY WORK IF YOU CAN'T GET PAID WORK

This applies to anyone who doesn't work – from school children or school leavers to adults out of work for any reason.

Voluntary work can be done around other activities such as school work, children or applying for jobs. Volunteers can work in school term time, school holidays, evenings or weekends, depending on the nature of the organization. There might be a one-off event – run by your school, university, local community or workplace – that you could contribute to, or an ongoing voluntary position that you want to fill.

If you can't find relevant voluntary work, work shadowing with local companies is another possibility. Shadowing can be very useful if you know what sort of job you want: it allows you to get some relevant experience. If you're at school, don't just rely on the standard single week of work experience that schools encourage everyone to do during exam years. Show you are serious by organizing additional job shadowing at other times.

THINK ABOUT YOUR INTERESTS

If you play sports or belong to a club, can you get more involved helping to organize matches or events? If you don't belong to a club, is there something local you are interested in and can join? Not every club charges a subscription fee, so you don't have to break the bank.

You don't have to pursue your hobbies as part of a club, although a club background can make your interests seem more genuine and serious. This can help if you aren't working. Focus on what you really enjoy, what interests and motivates you. If you follow something half-heartedly, it will be apparent when you write or talk about it.

WHAT ABOUT TRAINING?

If you have the time, and if necessary, the money – think about relevant training courses you might do. When you apply for a job already able to type 40 words per minute, or are able to use Microsoft Word or Excel rather than just being great at surfing the net, you'll have a huge advantage over people who can't offer the same basic skills.

Self-help books can be useful and online courses are commonplace, making it easy to study in your own time if you have a computer at home. Even if you just enrol on a cookery course to keep your brother company, or learn auto maintenance so you can fix up your car for when you pass your test, it all shows you want to learn and are ready to spend time improving your skills.

Continued development at work is worth taking full advantage of. If you would need management skills or team leadership experience to do the job you'd like to move to, try to get support for relevant training or ask for a chance to take on extra responsibility at work.

Time management

It might seem like a lot of additional work to physically improve your employability rather than just enhancing it on paper through effective writing, but it can be time well spent – especially if you have the goal of a specific job in mind.

When not working full-time, improving your employability can help you to stay busy, keep a routine, and prove to prospective employers you really want to work and develop your skills. It also proves you can manage your time effectively.

Gaps in your Employment History will seem less meaningful if you can show you've spent your time wisely since your last job or contract. It's hard to write a positive story if the truth is that you've done nothing but sit in the pub since you were made redundant. If you have, change it now by doing something you can talk positively about.

However busy you already are, don't write off opportunities to improve your employability. If wanting to return to work full time after a career break to have a family, you'd need to manage your family responsibilities and childcare around your new job: prove to an employer you are already a skilled time manager by adding to your skills with an online course.

MOTIVATION

If you have been struggling with motivation, particularly after lots of rejections from employers, you may find the process of writing your CV can help you to get back on track.

Writing your generic CV might highlight obstacles to getting a job that weren't clear to you before. Past issues can be smoothed out through positive spin, but others – especially current issues – may require practical solutions that you need to work on. Identify the obstacles you need to overcome, the gaps you need to close, and ways you can do so. You may then find your motivation starts to build as you measure your progress against your new goals.

ONE THING TO REMEMBER

▶ If positive spin can't redeem the poorest aspects of your CV,
  you may need to take action.

18

Further resources

In this chapter you will find:
- *other resources to help you write a great CV and find the job you want*

Teach yourself CV writing online

Go to www.teachyourself.co.uk/cvwriting for further information including templates, sample CVs, quizzes and other useful tools to help you write your own CV.

The site also contains a range of up-to-date links to help you to:

▶ carry out research into employers
▶ understand job competencies
▶ find jobs online
▶ try out Europass CVs and other tools
▶ find the best recruitment agency
▶ access job-hunting sites and CV libraries
▶ know where to find legal advice on employment issues
▶ learn more about disability and employment.

Links are not printed here as they change regularly.

The CV Centre – online

Visit www.ineedacv.co.uk for articles, advice, templates and tools – or some valuable feedback in the form of a free CV review.

Teach Yourself books

Go to www.teachyourself.co.uk/range to order great books to teach yourself everything from interview technique and career management to computing skills, foreign languages and more.

Index

academic posts, *165*
academic publications
  example, *172–3*
accuracy (qualifications), *27*
achievements, *87, 130, 155, 243*
Achievements (CV section),
  84, 177
    examples, *178, 181*
    targeting for job/
      employer, *193–4*
action words, *64–6*
    'power', *102–6, 110*
    refining, *102, 115–16*
    why they matter, *100–2*
adaptability, *61*
address
    email, *22–3*
    postal, *21*
adjectives
    empty, *110*
    power, *108–9, 112*
    repetition of, *111–12*
Adobe PDF file format, *226*
analytical skills, *59–61*
    action words, *65*
    see also thinking skills
answerphone message, *21*
anti-discrimination law
    and disclosure, *23–4*
    and support for disability,
      25
application forms, *250–2*
applications
    automated scanning of,
      82, 226
    reason for, *197–8*

appraisals (testimonials),
  243–4
automated scanning, *226*
    of applications, *82*
    of CVs, *188–90*
    see also scannability
awkward issues, *147*

being prepared, *266*
benefits of writing own CV,
  3–8
brevity, need for, *82*
brief employment, handling,
  131–2
bullet points (employment
  history), *47*
    need for evidence, *48*
    selecting, *85–7*
    as SHORT examples, *79*
bulleted summary, *87–8*

Career History (CV section),
  28, 30
    see also employment
      history
checking
    company names, *245*
    proofreading, *220–1*
children and convictions, *141*
chronological CVs, *174–5*
    conversion to functional,
      176–82
    example, *177–80*
    targeting for job/
      employer, *191–3*
clubs (interests), *38*

communication skills, *53–4*
    action words, *64–5*
    own CV as proof of, *4*
communications industry, *170*
Companies House, *199*
company
    describing a, *29*
    researching the, *196, 199*
Competencies (CV section)
    example, *180–1*
    targeting for job/
      employer, *193*
competency statements, *252–3*
competition for jobs, *1–2*
computer spell checkers, *221–2*
computers
    and automated scanning,
      82
    for CV preparation, *161–2*
    and digital CVs, *226–7*
    and disability, *25*
    as research/study tool,
      164, 274
    as skill, *33, 57, 66, 264*
concerns book deals with, *3*
confidence before interview,
    255–8
contact details, *20–3, 262*
contract-based work, *29, 169*
consistency of style, *92–3, 108*
convictions, dealing with, *141–3*
copies, need to keep, *251, 256–7*
covering emails, *245, 246*
covering letters, *237–45, 246*
    and application forms,
      250–1
    example, *240–2*
    targeting, *246–50*
creativity and innovation (skill),
    57–8
    action words, *65*

Curriculum Vitae, *2*
CV
    and application form, *252*
    and covering letter, *242–5*
    improving your, *271–5*
    type to use, *174–6*
    what it is, *2–3*
    where it might end up, *26*
CV companies, *6–7, 11*
CV filtering, *83*
CV format (structure), *182–3*
    conversion between,
      176–82
    type to use, *174–6*
    see also presentation of CVs
CV maintenance, *260–6*
CV update checklist, *262–4*
CV writing, basic rules of, *100*
cynicism, *50*

defence industry, *170*
digital CVs (electronic files),
    160, 161–2, 226–7, 256
    and hyperlinks, *23*
    problems with, *225, 227*
diplomatic service, *168*
disability, *24–5, 145–6*
Disability Discrimination Act, *25*
dyslexia, *205, 225*

editing up/down, *253*
education, *26–8*
Education (CV section)
    and specific industries,
      169, 170
    updating, *263*
elderly and convictions, *141*
electronic CV file *see* digital CVs
electronics industry, *170*
email address, *22–3*
emails, covering, *245, 246*

employability, enhancing, *271–5*
employer
    criticism of, *139–40*
    describing an, *29*
    issues with previous, *139–40*
employment
    brief, *131–2*
    gaps in, *126–8, 137–8, 146, 182*
    temporary, *29, 129–30*
    see also unemployment
employment history
    listing job responsibilities,
      31–5
    listing paid work, *28–30*
    voluntary work, *30–1*
Employment History
  (CV section)
    bullet point structure, *47–8*
    example entry, *9*
    questions to build, *48–52*
    targeting for job/
      employer, *191–2*
    updating, *262–3*
employment tribunals, *140*
empty adjectives, *110*
engineering industry, *168–9*
enthusiasm, need for, *164*
Europass, *168, 230–1*
exaggeration, *118–19*
examples (in book), meaning of
  'good, better, best', *51*
examples (own)
    checking strength, *77–9*
    converting into Summary,
      84–7
    in covering letter, *243*
    SHORTlisting, *69–79*

face to face, discussing, *143, 147*
factsheet, *46*
    adding examples to, *63, 64*

    adding highlights to, *93*
    into generic CV, *98, 160*
    refining action words, *102*
    SHORTlisting examples,
      69–79
feedback, incorporating, *264–5*
fields, *165*
    see also industries
filenames (digital CVs), *226–7*
files *see* digital CVs
finance (responsibility), *32–3*
first job, *30*
first person ('I'), *89–93*
flexibility (skill), *61–2*
    action words, *66*
font
    choice of, *208–9, 212–13*
    size/spacing/effects,
      209–11, 213
format of CVs (presentation),
  224–31
    see also CV format
functional CVs, *175–6*
    conversion to, *176–82*
    example, *180–2*
    and gaps, *127, 182*
    and specific industries,
      168, 169
    targeting for job/
      employer, *193*
Further Skills (CV section), *264*
    targeting for job/
      employer, *192*
    see also Skills
further skills and training,
  36–7

gaps in employment, *126–8, 182*
    redundancy example,
      137–8
    rules for explaining, *146*

gender and abbreviated
  names, *20*
generic CV, *160–1*
generic skills, *52–63*
graduates, *30, 39, 64, 169, 170*
gross misconduct, *121*

health, *24–5*
  see also disability; illness
highlights (skills examples),
  84, 93
home phone numbers, *21*
Honest examples, *71*
honest spin, *125–46*
  and language, *146–7*
  using, *132–3*
  see also positive spin
honesty, *122*
  and confidence, *258*
hybrid CVs, *176*
  and gaps, *182*
hyperlinks in documents, *23*

identity fraud, *26*
illness, handling long-term,
  143–5
impact, estimating own, *73–4*
industries
  expectations, *163–4, 165–71*
  need for enthusiasm, *164*
  summaries, *164*
industry-specific targeting,
  163–83
initiative (skill), *58–9*
  action words, *65*
innovation *see* creativity
interests, *38–9, 122, 274*
Interests (CV section), *39, 122, 264*
  targeting for job/
    employer, *192–3*
international dialling codes, *22*

interpersonal skills, *54–5*
  action words, *65*
interviews
  confidence before, *255–8*
  repeated refusal of, *2*
IT industry, *167–8*

jargon, *83*
  job titles as, *155*
  rules for, *151–5*
  what it is, *149–51*
job adverts
  and scanning software,
    188–90
  responding to, *185–8*
job descriptions, *50*
  versus responsibilities,
    51–2
job requirements (skills),
  121–2, 186–8, 194
job responsibilities, *31–5*
  proving competence, *50–1*
  versus descriptions, *51–2*
job titles, *48–9, 155*

Key Skills (CV section), *84, 169*
  example, *180–1*
  see also Skills; Summary
knowledge constraints
  (employers'), *83*

language and honest spin, *146–7*
layout of CV, *207–22*
learning (responsibility), *35*
leaving things out, *122, 132*
legal profession, *170–1*
legibility of CV, *207–13*
length
  of specialist CVs, *171–4*
  of targeted CVs, *194*
letters, covering, *237–45, 246–50*

lies, *118–21*
    and exaggeration, *118–19*
    and *The Apprentice* affair,
    120
    see also honest spin
line spacing, *210*
long-term illness, handling,
    143–5

management speak, *100*
manager, work as, *29*
market, researching the, *195–6*
medical positions, *166–7*
Microsoft Word
    CV preparation in, *23,*
    111–12, 160, 161, 226
    as skill, *37, 274*
mobile numbers, *21*
money (responsibility), *32–3*
motivation (skill), *58*
    action words, *65*
    improving, *275*

name, *19–20*
nationality, *168, 169*
negotiation (skill), *62–3*
    action words, *66*
nicknames, *20*
non-native speaker, *20*

Objective (CV section), *166, 170,*
    171, 245, 262
    examples, *180, 198*
    and personal statements,
    253
omissions *see* leaving things out
original certificates, need for,
    27–8
out of work
    employment gaps, *126, 146,*
    272

    story about, *132, 137–8, 143*
    voluntary work while,
    38, 273
    see also redundancy;
    unemployment
Outcome of examples, *72–4*
outcomes, realistic-sounding,
    75
overseas, coming to UK from,
    167
overseas applications, *22, 168,*
    229
    see also Europass

paper, CVs on, *224–6*
password protection of online
    CVs, *172*
past tense versus present,
    107–8
people (responsibility), *32*
personal details, *19–22, 229*
personal information, *23–6*
personal referees, *41*
personal security, *25–6*
    and online CVs, *172*
personal statement, *252–3*
    own CV as, *5–6*
personal trainer, own CV as, *5*
plain English, need for, *83*
podcast CVs, *227*
positive spin, *146, 275*
    and confidence, *257–8*
    see also honest spin
postal address, *21*
power, refining/adding, *115–16*
power action words, *102–6*
power adjectives, *108–9*
    repetition of, *112*
power versus word count,
    112–15
power words, use of, *110*

present tense versus past, *107–8*

presentation of CVs, *204*
    format, *224–31*
    layout, *207–22*

prioritizing essentials, *81–93*

prison terms, dealing with, *140–3*

problem areas
    convictions, *141–3*
    employment, *126–32*
    gap after redundancy, *136–9*
    long-term illness, *143–5*
    prison terms, *140–3*
    time to find first job, *133–6*

problem solving (skill), *56–7*
    action words, *65*

'professional development', *36*

professional qualifications and memberships, *36, 263*

professional referees, *40*

professionally-written CVs, *6–8, 11, 160–1*

Profile (CV section), *84, 262*
    examples, *177–8, 208–12*
    and personal statements, *253*
    and specific industries, *166, 169*
    targeting for job/ employer, *191*
    see also Summary

project-based work, *29, 167–8, 169*
    and functional CVs, *175–6*

proof
    and confidence, *256–7*
    of fitness despite illness, *145*
    of qualifications, *27*
    of skills, *48*
    of UK residence, *26*
    and use of adjectives, *109–10*

proofreading (checking), *220–1, 245*

prose summary, *88–9*

qualifications
    accuracy and proof, *27*
    Europass supplements, *231*
    outside education and employment, *36–7*
    professional, *36*
    see also education

Qualifications (CV section), *168, 263*

quality control, *220–2*

readability of CVs, *204–5, 216–20*

realistic assessment, own CV as, *7–8*

Realistic examples, *74–5*

reason for applying, *197–8*

reason for leaving, *139*

recruitment agencies
    CVs, rewriting by, *82, 108, 161*
    and feedback, *265*
    job of, *82*
    and jargon, *151*
    as source of advice, *183*

redundancy
    as bad luck, *137*
    gap after, *136–9*
    and voluntary work, *30–1*
    see also out of work; unemployment

references
    for new job, *39–42*
    from previous jobs, *243–4*

rehabilitation of offenders, 140–1
relevance, need for, 82, 194
repetition, avoiding, 111–12
research posts, 165
Research Skills (CV section) and legal profession, 170–1
responsibilities, realistic-sounding, 74–5
reverse chronological CVs see chronological CVs
reverse date order, 27, 28, 174
rewriting CV for each job, 11

sales job titles, examples of, 49
scannability (by human), 213–16
    see also automated scanning
school leavers, 38, 39, 41, 64, 273
screening
    and lies, 119, 121
    of references, 42
sectors/segments, 165
    see also industries
security see personal security
security clearance, 169
security screening, 42
sending out your CV, 236
sentence length, 217–19
SHORTlisting examples, 69–79
sick people and convictions, 141
skills, 47–67
    computer as, 33, 57, 66, 264
    five priority, 84–7
    job requirements, 121–2, 186–8, 194
    Microsoft Word as, 37, 274
    thinking, 34–5
    writing, own CV as proof of, 4
    see also further skills

Skills (CV section), 84, 168, 169, 177
    targeting for job/employer, 193
    see also Key Skills; Summary
specialist CVs, length of, 171–4
Specific examples, 70–1
speculative applications, 190–1
    covering letters/emails for, 246
spell checkers, 221–2
spent convictions, 141–2
spin
    honest, 125–47
    positive, 146, 257–8, 275
SPIN acronym, 132–3
statements, 252–3
'story', working on own, 133–9
stretching see exaggeration
Summary (CV section), 84, 182
    bulleted, 87–8
    example, 86–7
    prose, 88–9
    and specific industries, 166, 169, 170–1
    see also Key Skills; Profile; Skills
systems use (responsibility), 33–4

targeted CV, 163
targeting, 160–2
    covering letters, 244–5, 246–50
    different industries, 163–83
    employers, 194
    jobs, 185–94
teaching experience example, 173–4
teaching positions, 166

teams (interests), *38*
telephone number, *21–2*
temp *see* temporary employment
templates
    CV, *204, 214*
    Europass, *230*
    letter, *245*
temporary employment
    handling, *129–30*
    and length of history, *29*
tense, present versus past, *107–8*
testimonials, *243*
text alignment, *211–12, 213*
thinking skills (responsibility), *34–5*
    see also analytical skills
third person ('he', 'she'), *89–93*
time constraints (employers'), *81–2*
time management (skill), *55–6*
    action words, *65*
    improving, *275*
time needed to write CV, *11–12*
time to find first job, *133–6*
Training (CV section), *263*
    see also further skills
training (responsibility), *35*
training courses, *37, 137, 274*
Transferable examples, *76–7*
transferable skills *see* generic skills
'trying to', never use, *107*

UK
    proof of residence, *25*
    working in the, *167, 169*
    see also Europass

unemployment
    activities during, *137*
    and convictions, *141–2*
    gaps left by, *30–1, 146*
    and updating CV, *262, 271*
    and voluntary work, *30–1*
    see also out of work; redundancy
unspent convictions, *142–3*
unusual names, *20*

video CVs, *227–9*
voicemail, *21*
voluntary work, *30–1, 38, 145, 273*

weakness, not writing own CV as, *8*
web link to online CV, *172*
word count versus power, *112–15*
word length, *216–17*
work experience, *30, 145, 164, 263*
work for under-16s, *272–3*
Work History (CV section), *28, 30*
    see also employment history
work phone numbers, *21*
work shadowing, *273*
writing own CV
    basic rules of, *100*
    and confidence, *255–6*
    to cut costs, *6–7*
    when to start, *12–13, 272*
writing skills, own CV as proof of, *4*